Eureka! The art of co-creating the new YOU
Through science, spirituality, and a new quantum alchemy
A fusion for you evolution ©

Copyright © 2024 Miliza De Soto

First Edition: March, 2024
Windermere, Florida USA

ISBN: 979-8-9904791-1-1 Paperback
ISBN: 979-8-9904791-2-8 E-book

Editor in Chief: Carol Tietsworth
Proofread and Final Revision: Carol Tietsworth
Translations: Miliza De Soto
Cover Design: Luis Perozo
Back Cover Design: Cesar Aybar
Editorial Design: Cesar Aybar - www.cesaybar.com
Book Formatting: Alberto Martin - www.maquetadores.org
Art Director and Graphic Design: Cesar Aybar

www.milizadesoto.com

Legal Notice:

All rights reserved. No part of this book may be reproduced, distributed, or transmitted in any form or by any means, including photocopying, recording, or other electronic or mechanical methods, without the prior written permission of the author, except in the case of brief quotations embodied in critical reviews and certain other noncommercial uses permitted by copyright law.
For permissions requests or any inquiries, please contact: Miliza De Soto.
miliza@milizadesoto.com

This is an original work of Miliza De Soto.
All trademarks and registered trademarks mentioned herein are the property of their respective owners.

Thank you for respecting the hard work of the author.

EUREKA!

The art of co-creating the new YOU

Through science, spirituality and a new quantum alchemy

A fusion for your evolution

Miliza De Soto

Prologue

In the pages ahead, you're stepping into the chapters of my life—a journey spanning decades, marked by exploration, research, and experiences that have fundamentally shifted how I see the world. This book is more than just words; it's the product of a burning desire to unravel the very essence of life and figure out how to live it to the fullest.

Over the years, I've been on a fascinating ride into the mysteries of the human mind and heart. It's been a journey of studying, researching, and experiencing. I've been there for many individuals on their quest for self-discovery and personal fulfillment, witnessing transformations and the ignition of human potential.

My pride knows no bounds when I think of my children, Paola "Lola" and Nicholas. They've carved their paths in exploring the mind and reality. Paola dives deep into studying the mind, emotions, and tireless research. Nicholas immerses himself in the profound realms of quantum physics and parallel universes. And then there's my niece Johanna, her curiosity and dedication to learning more, especially in medicine and science, filling me with pride.

These individuals are not just family; they're beacons of inspiration in my life. This book is my way of paying tribute to their relentless pursuit of knowledge and unwavering love.

You'll find teachings and a collection of my passion, experiences, and wisdom accumulated over the years here. I attempt to distill what it means to live a purposeful, joyous, and authenticity-filled life.

I hope these pages become a guiding light for you. May they equip you with tools to face challenges, transform your thoughts, and unfurl your wings toward realizing your dreams. Let this book constantly remind you that you can live an extraordinary life.

May these words kindle a fire within you, urging you to embrace your authenticity, discover your limitless potential, and dance to the rhythm of your melody. Consider this book a tribute to all those dedicated to the journey toward fulfillment and vibrant life—a gift to help you light up your inner brilliance and shine in all your splendor.

Welcome to this expedition of self-discovery, evolution, and transformation! May these pages steer you toward a realm of boundless possibilities, inspiring you to craft the life you deserve.

With eternal gratitude,

Miliza De Soto

Dedication

This book is dedicated to those craving more, feeling the inner pull toward a fuller, more conscious, and more positive life. To those brave enough to confront their fears and delve into the depths of their being. To all who've trusted in me and in themselves to embark on this journey.

To Paola, Nicholas, and Johanna

Introduction

In the vastness of the cosmos, we call home, an unfathomable mystery has intrigued humanity since time immemorial. It's the mystery that hides behind every star, whispers in the wind, and beats in our hearts—the grand mystery of the universe, the intricate fabric of reality that envelops our existence.

Throughout the centuries, we've sought answers to profound questions: Who are we? Why are we here? What is the purpose of life? These questions are threads in a veil that shrouds the face of the universal mystery. In these pages, we embark on a collective journey to unveil that veil and explore answers that transcend our everyday understanding.

This book invites you to look beyond the familiar, question entrenched beliefs, and open your mind to the vastness of the universe and its infinite possibilities. As we progress, we'll navigate territories where science and spirituality entwine, where the mind and matter merge in a cosmic dance.

As we dive into the heart of this grand mystery, we'll discover how our perceptions, beliefs, and thoughts shape our reality. We'll explore consciousness, quantum physics, and the miracles that unfurl when hearts and minds open. Throughout this journey, we'll lift the veil on the universe's mystery and unveil the magic within ourselves.

In the pages ahead, we'll explore concepts tied to co-creation, the universe, and spirituality. These ideas may wear different names based on beliefs—whether the higher force we call God, the quantum field, or the source. Feel free to assign it a name aligned with your beliefs; what matters is the meaning behind these words and how they aid in understanding your potential as a creative being. This book doesn't aim to define or limit; it seeks to open you to infinite possibilities. I invite you to navigate this journey and find your truth in the cosmos's mystery.

Fundamentals of Quantum Alchemy

Welcome to an extraordinary odyssey at the heart of Quantum Alchemy. This discipline intertwines science and spirituality, blending quantum physics with ancient wisdom and uniting mind and matter in a cosmic dance of limitless possibilities. Within these pages, we'll delve into the foundations of this modern alchemy and explore how you can apply these principles to manifest your deepest desires.

Quantum alchemy surpasses abstract theory; it's a way to comprehend and experience reality. It rests on the premise that we are co-creators of our universe, and our perceptions and beliefs mold the reality we inhabit. This amalgamation of ancient wisdom and cutting-edge science equips us with tools to reshape our lives in ways that once seemed implausible.

We'll unravel pivotal concepts forming the bedrock of Quantum Alchemy:

Consciousness as Creator: Uncover how your consciousness is the very source of your reality. Your perception, thoughts, and emotions weave the tapestry of your life.

Quantum Physics in Everyday Life: Explore how the tenets of quantum physics apply to our daily experiences and empower us to effect profound changes.

The Magic of Belief and Expectation: Understand how your beliefs and expectations act as magnets, drawing experiences and situations aligned with your deepest thoughts.

The Dance of Co-Creation: Immerse yourself in the art of co-creating with the universe. Learn to align your desires and actions with universal energy to manifest your dreams.

The Power of Imagination and Perception: Delve into how imagination and evident perception can be potent tools for personal transformation.

The Science of Gratitude and Reception: Grasp how gratitude and the ability to receive are fundamental to opening yourself to abundance and fulfillment.

As you progress through this book, practical exercises, inspiring examples, and effective techniques await you— tools to integrate these fundamentals into your daily life.

You stand at the threshold of a journey—from comprehending the mind and reality to mastering conscious co-creation. Get ready to discover the magic within and unveil the universe's secrets.

This lays the foundation for the new alchemy—a fusion of ancient wisdom and contemporary science, providing you with keys to design the life you've always yearned for. Are you prepared to unlock the door to the extraordinary?

1

The Power of Consciousness

"Imagination is the tool that turns dreams into facts. When we paint with colors of possibility, we create a mural of opportunities"

Consciousness is the blank canvas on which we paint the portrait of our reality. A palette of thoughts, emotions, and perceptions shapes what we experience. Perception is the key that opens the door to a world of possibilities.

What we perceive as truth becomes our reality. Our mind, a tireless creator, transforms what we believe into what we live. Imagination is the tool that turns dreams into reality. When we paint with colors of possibility, we create a mural of opportunities. There are no limits, only those we create in our minds. Expectation is the guiding thread weaving the tapestry of your story.

When we eagerly anticipate what is to come, we weave a narrative rich in achievements and joys.

The new personality emerges like a phoenix from our aspirations. With every thought and feeling, we shape a renewed "self." Transformation begins in the mind and manifests in every aspect of life. As captains of our destiny, we design a vibrant and full potential tomorrow.

Every step we take brings us closer to that vision. As we navigate the stream of consciousness, we embrace our creator role. With every elevated thought, every emotion of gratitude, and every belief in the possible, we chart our destiny among the stars.

2

A Coherent Signal

Brain and Body in Harmony

"Anticipation and mental preparation are like the prelude to an epic performance. Mentally practicing over and over is essential to create a perfect symphony of reality"

Imagine your mind and body as a perfectly orchestrated symphony. Every thought, every emotion, every heartbeat resonates in a unique melody. But how can our perceptions and emotions affect the music of our physiology? The effect of this intimate dance is more profound than we could have imagined.

Our body is not just a container for our mind but a canvas on which every thought paints its vibrant hue. From the genetic level to the beating of our heart, each cell is influenced by the emotional composition we emit.

This intricate link between mind and body is astonishing. Genetic changes can occur in response to emotions, affecting the expression of our genes. Imagine emotion as a conductor guiding our cells in a symphony of health and well-being or in a dissonant melody of disease and discomfort. Embracing a future event before it materializes in the present is crucial. Anticipation and mental preparation are like the prelude to an epic performance. Mentally practicing over and over is essential to create a perfect symphony of reality.

In the present moment, all possibilities lie within our reach. In the field of potential reality, all our choices exist simultaneously. When we remain present, we transcend time and space. We can turn any potential into reality through the mastery of our minds.

3

Inner Illumination

Weaving Reality

*"Imagine you are an alchemist, a wizard of the mind.
You have the power to turn lead into gold and adversity
into triumph"*

Picture each thought as a seed you plant in the vast garden of existence. Like the life-giving sun, your mind nurtures these seeds, coaxing them to grow and bloom in the garden of reality. Perception acts as the key, turning these seeds into the bountiful harvest of your life.
Imagine yourself as an alchemist, a sorcerer of the mind. You possess the power to turn lead into gold, to transform adversity into triumph. Your mind serves as the enchanted cauldron where you blend the ingredients of your thoughts and emotions, conjuring your unique reality.

The alchemy of transformation begins with conscious perception. It's an introspective journey, observing how thoughts intertwine with emotions. Each thought and emotion weave a strand in the tapestry of our lives. To consciously weave this fabric is an act of true mastery.

The heart of transformation beats in perception. Like a blank canvas, life awaits the strokes of your mind's brush. Do you see adversity as an insurmountable obstacle, or is it an opportunity for growth? Are your dreams distant and unattainable, or are they goals waiting for you to conquer? Perception molds reality by shaping the very chemistry of your brain and body. Altering your perception induces changes in your body's chemistry. Your brain responds to the dance of your thoughts and emotions, creating neural patterns that echo your perception and influencing how you engage with the world.
Conscious perception empowers you to choose how you relate to reality. Challenges can morph into opportunities and adversity into triumph. By reshaping your perception, you redefine how your mind interprets events, thus transforming your responses.
Ultimately, you are the artist of your reality. Through your thoughts and emotions, you wield the power to shape your experience. Being aware of your perception and choosing how you interpret the world turns you into the master of your destiny.

4

Life by Design

Infusing Emotion into Creation

"Belief is the spark that ignites the flame of manifestation"

Envision your life as an empty canvas, eagerly awaiting the strokes of your thoughts, feelings, and beliefs. In this chapter, we embark on a profound exploration of the transformative practice of breathing life into your dreams through emotion and belief.

Life unfolds as a continuous creation, where every thought harbored is a seed capable of blossoming into your reality. Your mind serves as the atelier where you meticulously design and construct the vibrant tapestry of your life. Yet, merely holding a thought isn't sufficient; it needs the infusion of the right emotion to spring to life in the tangible world.

Think of a sculptor molding clay—each movement of their hands and every nuance they add to the clay expresses their vision and emotion. Similarly, as you craft your life, your thoughts are the malleable clay, and your feelings are the skilled hands shaping it.

Here's the clandestine truth: it's not merely about contemplating what you want. **"Belief is the spark that ignites the flame of manifestation."** If the flame of belief doesn't flicker, attempting to manifest your dream is akin to trying to kindle a fire with damp wood. Belief activates an internal force that sets the dream-weaving process into motion.

It's as if life responds to your expectations. Immersing yourself in the emotion of already having what you desire compels reality to mirror that emotional state. This underscores why your present mental and emotional state is the cornerstone upon which you construct your creation.

Remember, you are the craftsman of your life. You play the roles of architect, designer, and alchemist in shaping your experiences.

Life and emotion dance together, and once you grasp this symbiotic connection, you become a magician capable of transmuting dreams into reality.

Take a moment to reflect: How would you feel if you'd already achieved your deepest desire? Picture your life as it is now with that fulfillment. Savor that feeling; let it wash over you. This enchantment breathes life into your thoughts, crafting the reality you crave.

Thus, adhering to this philosophy of life design, we'll explore how your awareness and emotions are the vital ingredients for shaping your world. This unfolds as a thrilling journey of conscious creation—a metamorphosis of your life from within.

5

Learning to Let Go

It's a Lifelong Process

"Releasing is an art, a dance of the mind and spirit. By leaving behind obsolete beliefs and emotional burdens, you make space for new experiences to unfold"

Every day, renew your determination to release the past and shed any worries. This paves the way for fresh, healthy choices that will make your life extraordinary. When you release thoughts, emotions, and behaviors that have held you back, you unleash your life force, radiating a bright and beautiful vibration for all to see.

Imagine your life as a canvas awaiting your masterful strokes. Just as an artist removes excess paint from the canvas, letting go of what no longer serves, you must also release old patterns, fears, and doubts. These are just smears on the canvas of your potential.

Releasing is an art, a dance of the mind and spirit. Leaving behind outdated beliefs and emotional baggage makes room for new experiences to unfold. It's a journey of self-discovery and empowerment, a constant and fluid process. When you free yourself from the chains of the past, you allow your energy to flow freely in the present. It's like a river sweeping away debris, making space for new life. The act of letting go is an affirmation that you are ready for growth, transformation, and renewal.

Remember, the journey of release isn't about perfection; it's about progress. Every step you take toward letting go is a step toward your true self. Embrace the challenges that arise because they are opportunities for growth and expansion.

By releasing the old and making room for the new, you align with the abundant flow of life. You become a vessel of light, radiating positivity and vitality. Releasing isn't an end; it's a beginning. It's a commitment to your well-being and the continual unveiling of your highest potential.

You invite fresh energy, new perspectives, and limitless possibilities into your life through release.

Embrace the journey with an open heart and a willing spirit. As you let go, you make space for miracles to materialize and open the door to a life of infinite potential.

6

Physics of Consciousness

The Science of Possibilities

"Every thought, every emotion, every intention we harbor in our minds emits a signal that reverberates through the interconnected network of reality"

Consciousness, that mysterious force residing within us, is the engine propelling reality. In the vast ocean of the universe, consciousness is the compass guiding our perceptions and experiences. Through consciousness, we explore the limits of what is possible and create our own version of reality.

The physics of consciousness is a marvelous exploration of the infinite possibilities at the very heart of our existence. It immerses us in the quantum world, where subatomic particles dance in a cosmic ballet of probabilities and potentialities. Here, the laws of traditional physics give way to the more flexible and ever-changing rules of the quantum realm.

Consciousness is more than a mere observer; it is an active participant in the dance of creation. Every thought, every emotion, every intention we harbor in our minds sends a signal that reverberates through the interconnected network of reality. Our perceptions not only influence our personal experience but also affect the fabric of the universe itself.

Imagine consciousness as an invisible spiderweb connecting all things. Each thread of thought and emotion we weave in this interdimensional web creates a unique pattern reflected in our reality. When we change our consciousness, we alter the pattern, thus changing our experience of existence.

The physics of consciousness teaches us that we are the architects of our experience. Our thoughts and emotions are the tools with which we sculpt our reality. By understanding the profound interaction between the mind and the universe, we embrace our role as co-creators of existence. **The science of possibilities invites us to transcend the limits of traditional perception and explore the vast field of potentialities before us.** Here, events are not predetermined but shaped by consciousness itself. Every choice we make, every intention we hold, has the power to transform our world.

Just as an artist paints on a blank canvas, we paint on the

canvas of reality with the brushes of our consciousness. Our thoughts are the colors we choose, and our emotions are the strokes we make. Every day, every moment, we are creating the masterpiece that is our life.

The physics of consciousness reminds us that we are not merely passive spectators in this vast cosmic spectacle. We are active participants and co-creators of our narrative. As we explore the depths of our consciousness, we open doors to new dimensions of experience and potential.

7

The Key to Conscious Creation

Mastering Perception

"What we perceive is not a direct representation of objective reality but a subjective interpretation colored by our internal landscape"

In the intricate symphony of life, perception takes the lead, shaping the rhythm of reality. How we see ourselves and the world becomes the melody of our experiences. It's not a passive observation but a dynamic force molding thoughts, emotions, and, ultimately, our reality.

Think of perception as a kaleidoscope, turning to reveal different colors and patterns, creating a unique view. Similarly, our perception filters reality through beliefs, biases, and experiences.

Perception isn't confined to external senses; it's a multidimensional experience involving thoughts, emotions, and bodily sensations. What we perceive isn't an exact representation but a subjective interpretation colored by our internal landscape.

Thoughts and emotions weave into perception, forming a loop that influences our mental state and external experiences. Positive perception triggers positive emotions, reinforcing the positive perception. This cycle perpetuates and amplifies our reality.

To tap into the power of perception, we must first explore our internal landscape, uncovering beliefs and thought patterns shaping our view. By shining awareness on perception, we refine our understanding of reality.
Crucially, perception isn't fixed; it's a malleable force we can consciously direct. By choosing what aspects to focus on and shifting perspective, we transform how we experience reality. This is the key to conscious creation.
Understanding the intimate connection between perception, thought, and emotion gives us a master key to reality. Altering perception changes thought and emotion patterns, modifying our experience. This isn't fantasy; it's the physics of consciousness in action.

As we delve into perception, we realize reality is a canvas waiting for the brushstrokes of our consciousness. Each shift opens portals of possibility, leading to unexplored territories.

8

The Magic of Anticipation

The Power to "Believe to Create"

"The magic of anticipation is not simply a passive desire but an active attitude of believing something is possible"

On life's canvas, anticipation is the brush bringing our reality to life. Each stroke of belief transforms the canvas into our masterpiece. The power of expectation isn't just abstract; it shapes reality around us.

Anticipation fuels the engine of manifestation. Fervent belief generates energy propelling our experience. Positive expectations attract aligned circumstances; negative expectations create a magnetic field for experiences in tune with those vibrations.

This isn't just a mental game; it's grounded in quantum mechanics. Thoughts and beliefs emit a frequency of interacting with the environment. Hopes are seeds in reality's field, growing what we've sown.

Anticipation isn't passive wishing but an active belief that something is possible. Expecting with certainty activates a creation process beyond the conscious mind—our subconscious works in the shadows to make expectations a reality.

We cultivate certainty and faith in our dreams to harness this power, focusing on the desired outcome. Positive expectation guides us through storms, maintaining the vision of what we wish to achieve.

After planting seeds of hope, we water them with appropriate emotion and energy. Emotions act as nutrients, allowing the seed to grow in our reality. We feel with passion and conviction that our longings will be fulfilled, which is essential for materialization.

Anticipation is a dance between mind and heart, aligning thoughts, emotions, and desires. It's a golden ticket to the theater of creation, witnessing the spectacle of our experiences.

In the river of desires, every belief and every positive expectation brings us closer to turning dreams into reality.

On this journey, we're not just spectators but masters of creation.

9

The Quantum Dance

When Energy Meets Intention

"The energy behind our intentions expands through the quantum field, creating patterns that shape events in our lives"

In the mesmerizing realm of quantum physics, the interplay of energy and intention orchestrates the grand symphony of reality. Just like a conductor guides an orchestra, our intentions steer the energetic particles that weave the intricate fabric of existence. This dance knows no bounds of time or space; it transcends the limitations of the material world.

Quantum physics unveils a universe where the observed and the observer are intricately entwined. Our thoughts, intentions, and beliefs shape the behavior of subatomic particles, a phenomenon known as the observer effect—where observation alters the outcome. Envision reality as a pristine canvas awaiting the artistry of our intentions. Each intention is a brushstroke on the canvas of existence. The energy propelling our intentions ripples through the quantum field, crafting patterns that mold the events in our lives.

Quantum dance is a harmonious co-creation. We are not mere spectators; we actively partake in shaping reality. Intentions are seeds sown in the fertile soil of the universe. We nurture these seeds with focused attention and aligned emotion, allowing them to sprout and bloom. The essence of quantum dance is alignment—syncing thoughts, emotions, and intentions with the desired outcome. When these elements harmonize, a potent resonance is born, amplifying energy and hastening the process of materialization. It's akin to tuning an instrument to produce the perfect melody.

In quantum dance, time and space become pliable. We can transcend the constraints of linear time, delving into the potential of the present moment. This signifies that our intentions can reach backward and forward in time, influencing events that have already unfolded or are yet to come. This concept might stretch conventional thinking, but it harmonizes with insights from ancient wisdom traditions. Mystics and sages have long grasped the interconnectedness of all things and the potency of intention in shaping reality. Now, science is catching up to these ageless insights.

Stepping onto the quantum dance floor, we become choreographers and dancers. Our intentions set the rhythm, and our energy propels the movement. Each step in the dance of intention is a stride toward our envisioned reality. With each move, we rewrite the script of our lives. Quantum dance beckons us to liberate ourselves from the material world's confinements and explore the universe's boundless potential. It's an odyssey into the frontiers of consciousness, where thoughts aren't fleeting whims but foundational building blocks of creation.

10

The Power of Cognition and Imagination

"Imagination is a door to unexplored worlds. When we use our imagination to visualize what we want to materialize, we take the first step toward creation"

In the theater of the mind, cognition and imagination join hands to breathe life into the narrative of our reality. How we perceive and interpret becomes the cornerstone upon which we construct our experiences, shaping our perception of the universe and ourselves. It's a captivating dance between the external world and our inner world.

Cognition is the lens through which we view the world, filtering reality into a mosaic of colors and shapes. But here, we contemplate the spectrum entirely: our perceptions aren't neutral reflections of objective reality. Instead, they are subjective interpretations woven with our beliefs, past experiences, and emotions.

Imagine gazing at a piece of art. Two individuals can behold the same painting and evoke entirely different reactions. One might feel inspired and moved, while another might find it incomprehensible or displeasing. This illustrates how our internal states and personal narratives sculpt our perceptions.

Here's the essence: our cognitions don't just mirror our current reality; they can also mold it. When we perceive something in a particular light, that perception influences our response and engagement with the world. It's as if our perception is a brush, painting strokes on the canvas of reality.

Here is where imagination enters the stage. Imagination is the mental workshop where dreams take form. It's where we conceive and explore possibilities before they materialize in the tangible world. Our imagination enables us to venture into potential futures and rehearse different scenarios.

Imagination is a portal to uncharted realms. When we employ our imagination to visualize what we wish to materialize, we take the inaugural step toward creation. Yet, this isn't solely a mental exercise; it's a process engaging our entire being.

When we imagine with emotion and energy, we dispatch a signal to the cosmos.

"The power of imagination lies in its ability to alter our energetic vibration." Our energy aligns with that vision when we imagine with precision and emotion. This shifts our frequency, attracting situations and circumstances resonating with that energy. Essentially, we're sowing the seeds of the reality we aspire to create.

The interplay between cognition and imagination is dynamic. Our perceptions influence how we imagine the future, and our imaginations can reshape our cognitions. We can actively shape our reality by altering how we perceive things and visualizing fresh possibilities. This journey of conscious creation demands practice and sustained awareness. It compels you to challenge your constraining perceptions and cultivate the ability to envision what you haven't witnessed. In doing so, you're constructing bridges between your inner and external worlds, allowing the dance between cognition and imagination to evolve into a harmonious symphony.

Remember, you are the storyteller and protagonist of your tale. The way you choose to interpret the world and the images you paint in your mind possess the power to alter the trajectory of your life. As you sway in this dance of cognition and imagination, remember you hold the brush and face the blank canvas before you.

11

The Power of Focus and Belief

"Our beliefs are the foundations upon which we build our world perception. They are the lenses through which we interpret reality"

In the vast field of possibilities, attention, and belief act as guiding beacons shaping our experience. What we focus on and believe—becomes the backdrop of our reality, akin to tuning a radio to a specific station.

Focus is an excellent tool allowing us to direct our attention to a specific point, like adjusting a camera lens for a clear image. But what happens when our attention scatters in multiple directions? Reality becomes blurry and fragmented.

Here is where belief comes into play. Beliefs form the foundation upon which we construct our perception of the world. They are the lenses through which we interpret reality. If we believe in scarcity, we'll see evidence of it everywhere. If we believe in possibility and abundance, we'll begin identifying opportunities at every turn.

Belief is potent because it's self-fulfilling. When we staunchly believe in something, our mind seeks evidence to support that belief. We are creating a confirmation loop where our experiences reinforce what we believe. Our mind is a private detective searching for clues to confirm our theory.

But here's the twist: our beliefs aren't fixed. We can consciously choose beliefs that serve us and discard those that limit us. Imagine your beliefs are like outfits you can change according to the occasion. If an outfit doesn't fit well, there's no obligation to wear it.

By combining focus and belief, we create a powerful synergy. We send a clear signal to the universe when we focus on what we desire and underpin that focus with a solid conviction in possibility. We're communicating our willingness to receive what we seek.

This synergy works in the opposite direction as well. If we allow our attention to center on what we fear or don't want and support that attention with limiting beliefs, we send an equally clear signal. We're asking for more of what we don't desire.

The key is to take the helm of your attention and beliefs. In doing so, you become the captain of your ship. You can steer it toward calm, prosperous waters or turbulent, stormy seas. The choice is yours, and the tool is your conscious focus.

When you focus your attention and belief on what you want to create, you sow the seeds of the reality you yearn for. You're emitting a powerful signal to attract circumstances and opportunities resonating with your vibration. Like a magnet, your focus and belief will draw toward you that which you concentrate on.

As you progress on this journey of focus and belief, remember you are the director of your experience. You have the ability to change the channel of your attention and adjust your beliefs at any moment. As you move through this dance of focus and belief, remember you are creating your unique symphony in the vast cosmic choir.

12

The Power of Expectation and the New Reality

"The reality we experience directly reflects our perceptions, beliefs, and emotions"

In this immense canvas of creation, we are both the artist and the canvas. The reality we experience directly reflects our perceptions, beliefs, and emotions. As artists, we can paint on this canvas of possibilities with vibrant colors of intention and emotion.

Imagine reality as a blank canvas before you. Your mind is the brush, and your emotions are the pigments you'll use to create. With every thought and feeling, you're applying strokes to the canvas. And as you do, the canvas comes to life with your creations.

Yet here's the magical twist: the canvas isn't static or passive. It's in constant interaction with you. Every stroke you apply triggers a response from the canvas itself. If you paint strokes of love and gratitude, the canvas responds with bright and vibrant colors. The canvas reflects a darker palette if you paint strokes of fear and doubt.

Here is where conscious intention comes in—when you deliberately decide what you want to create on your canvas of reality, you're giving direction to your brush. Intention acts like the pattern guiding your movements and defining the image you're creating. It's like a movie script that sets the story's tone and message. But intention alone isn't enough. The strokes must also be infused with emotion. Emotions are the energy breathing life into your creations. Think of your emotions as the wind propelling your ship's sails in the ocean of possibilities. Your journey will be fluid and powerful if your emotions are strong and clear.

At this point, a disconnection often occurs. Often, we're so focused on what we want to create that we need to pay attention to how we feel in the process. If you paint with a brush loaded with doubts and anxiety, your creation will reflect those emotions. On the other hand, if you paint with a brush full of joy, passion, and confidence, your creation will resonate with those vibrations. It's not just about what you're painting but how you feel while doing it. Your emotions become the temperament of your brush and determine the quality of your strokes.

As the artist of your reality, you have the power to choose the colors and emotions you apply to your canvas. You can create landscapes of beauty and harmony or images of challenge and triumph. Every choice you make shapes the experience you're developing. Remember, the canvas of possibilities is infinite and versatile. No matter how many strokes you've applied in the past, you always have the opportunity to start anew. Every moment is a blank page you can paint with love and creativity: it's your decision.

13

Quantum Surprises

Harnessing the Power of the Unpredictable

"Instead of clinging to specific results or insisting on how our intentions should manifest, we can allow the universe to surprise us with its creativity"

In the infinite canvas of cosmic creation, quantum reality paints a fascinating landscape of surprises and possibilities. In the quantum world, the laws of causality and predictability often waver, making room for the unexpected and astonishing.

Think about this: at the quantum level, particles can exist in multiple states simultaneously. They are said to be in a state of superposition, where they can be particles and waves simultaneously. It means a particle can be in several places simultaneously until measured or observed, as mentioned before.

And here's the magic: when we observe a particle, its state collapses into a particular one. Most amazingly, this collapsed state seems to be influenced by our observation. In other words, consciousness gives the impression of playing a fundamental role in how the quantum world materializes.

The phenomenon is known as the collapse of the wave function and has puzzled scientists for decades. For us conscious creators, this interaction between consciousness and quantum reality reminds us of our power to influence the very fabric of existence.

So, how can we harness this power of the unpredictable in our lives? The key lies in an attitude of openness and acceptance. Instead of clinging to specific outcomes or insisting on how our intentions should manifest, we can allow the universe to surprise us with its creativity.

Quantum surprises remind us that our expectations can limit us. When we're willing to let go of our 'rigid expectations' and 'be open to any outcome,' we release the natural flow of creative energy. It can lead to outcomes more astonishing than we could ever have imagined. So, as you progress on this journey of conscious creation, remember that the quantum world is a dance partner willing to surprise you every step of the way. Embrace uncertainty with joy and curiosity, and watch how quantum surprises guide you into a realm of infinite possibilities.

14

The Energy of Atoms

Weaving the Tapestry of Reality

"Each atom is like a note in the score of life. Our thoughts, emotions, and actions generate vibrations that resonate with like-minded particles. When we align our energy with the frequency of what we want to manifest, we enter into creative resonance with the cosmos"

At the very heart of creation lies the intimate dance of atoms. These tiny builders of reality are like threads weaving the tapestry of our universe. Each atom vibrates with a unique energy and connects with other atoms in a cosmic ballet of interaction.

Imagine that blank canvas where each stroke is a dancing atom. Each atom has its vibration frequency, its song in the symphony of existence. When we observe reality at the subatomic level, we see that everything is energy in motion, constantly flowing and changing.

Quantum science tells us that even observers affect the observed. The simple act of observing an atom can change its behavior. It leads us to a fascinating truth: "We are active co-creators in this cosmic play." Our consciousness, intention, and energy influence how atoms interlace to form tangible reality.

This idea has been expressed in many spiritual and philosophical traditions. Ancient Hermetic wisdom speaks of the law of correspondence: "As above, so below." Suggests that the patterns and processes we observe in the universe are also reflected in our internal experience.

Each atom is like a note in the score of life. Our thoughts, emotions, and actions generate vibrations that resonate with like-minded atoms. When we align our energy with the frequency of what we want to manifest, we enter into a creative resonance with the cosmos.

But here's the magic: we could influence the atoms around us and also affect our atoms. Our body itself is a symphony of energy in constant motion. Every cell and molecule vibrates with the energy of our experiences, emotions, and thoughts.

The science of epigenetics tells us that our thoughts and emotions can directly affect the expression of our genes. It means we have the skill to influence our biology through consciousness. We can shape our reality from the inside out.

So, as we explore the depths of quantum reality, let's remember that we are conscious weavers of the tapestry of existence. Every thought, every emotion, every intention is a strand in this cosmic work.

As we adjust our vibrations and align with what we want to create, we are transforming the canvas of reality into a masterpiece of our own making.

15

The Symphony of Being

Integration and Transformation

"Transformation is the journey that takes us from where we are to where we want to be—it is the process of becoming an elevated version of oneself, letting go of what no longer serves us, and embracing new ways of being and living"

Each of us is a symphony in motion on the grand stage of life. We are a blend of experiences, emotions, thoughts, and desires weaving into a unique harmony. Yet, amidst the discord of existence, we might sometimes feel disconnected from our true essence.

Integration is the art of combining all the scattered parts of ourselves, harmonizing them into a coherent symphony.

It's akin to tuning the instruments of our mind, body, and spirit to play in perfect harmony. When integrated, we feel whole and aligned with our inner truth. Transformation is the journey that takes us from where we are to where we wish to be—it's the process of becoming an elevated version of ourselves, letting go of what no longer serves us, and embracing new ways of being and living.

Transformation is the inner alchemist that turns adversity into opportunity and darkness into light. The dance of integration and transformation is a sacred choreography. It demands self-awareness and courage to explore the parts of ourselves in the shadows. It requires the willingness to release old beliefs and patterns that have limited us. And it necessitates having a vision of what we want to create in our lives.

Integration and transformation are ongoing processes. There is no final destination; instead, there are layers and levels of constant discovery. As we ascend towards a new way of being, we may encounter resistance in the form of ingrained fears and comfort zones. But each challenge is an opportunity for growth.

Authenticity is the key to integration, transformation, and evolution. Being authentic means embracing all parts of ourselves: lights and shadows, strengths and vulnerabilities. As we fully accept ourselves, we release the energy trapped in denial and resistance. "Self-inquiry" is a powerful tool in this journey. Questions like Who am I? What do I want to create in my life? Guide us toward a profound understanding of ourselves and our deepest aspirations.

Each question invites us to explore, question, and create space for new answers.

Self-expression also plays a crucial role in integration and transformation. Finding creative ways to express our emotions and experiences allows us to release what has been trapped within us. Our inner voice echoes through art, music, writing, or movement. As we continue in the dance of integration and transformation, remember that we are the conductors of our symphony.

We have the power to choose the notes we want to play and the melodies we wish to create. As we tune into our authenticity and open ourselves to the possibility of transformation, we co-create a life that resonates with our deepest essence.

16

The Physics of Consciousness

The Universe of Possibilities and Probabilities

"Our deep consciousness, perception, and intentions can directly impact the reality we experience"

On the boundless stage of existence, physics and consciousness intertwine in a cosmic gala full of possibilities. Physics, the study of the laws governing the universe, and consciousness, the essence of human experience, converge at a point where reality and perception merge.

Modern physics offers a window into a world where the game's rules entirely differ from what we used to believe. We now know that scientists have discovered that at a subatomic level, particles can exist in multiple states at once, a phenomenon known as quantum superposition. It means that a particle can be in various places simultaneously and in different energy states.

Now, this concept challenges our conventional understanding of reality and leads us to question the very nature of existence.

It suggests a profound connection between the mind and matter, where consciousness is the passive spectator and an active participant in creating the cosmos.

In addition to quantum superposition, physics introduces us to the concept of quantum entanglement. Particles that have been entangled maintain an instantaneous connection even when separated by astronomical distances. No matter how far apart they are, a change in one particle's state instantly affects its entangled partner. Here, it raises the idea that space and time are not absolute barriers but rather "constructions of our limited perception."

Fascinating and enigmatic quantum physics challenges us to reconsider our relationship with the quantum field, where the known laws of reality bend and stretch, opening the door to a world of yet unexplored possibilities. It suggests that we are much more profoundly interconnected with everything around us than we imagined. Our consciousness, perception, and intentions can directly impact the reality we experience. The idea that we are passive observers in the cosmos crumbles, and in its place emerges the notion that we are active co-creators, influencing the very plot of the cosmos.

The physics of consciousness invites us to explore new horizons of possibilities. It challenges us to transcend the limitations of conventional perception and embrace the idea that reality is much more malleable than we believe.

As we delve into this exploration, we may discover that we are an integral part of the fabric of the universe, and our minds and hearts have the power to shape the reality we wish to see.

17

The Science of Consciousness

Unraveling the Threads of the Quantum Field

"Consciousness acts as the bridge that connects us to this vast matrix of possibilities. It is through consciousness that we translate energy waves into tangible experiences"

In the cosmic loom, consciousness is the golden thread that weaves the internal and external worlds together. The science of consciousness is like a kaleidoscope revealing hidden patterns that shape our reality. As we explore this science, we discover that we are more than mere spectators in the theater of life; we are the creators themselves.

Consciousness is like an antenna picking up signals from an invisible reality. Beyond what we see with our physical eyes, there is a vast ocean of energy and vibrations. Consciousness acts as the bridge connecting us to this enormous matrix of possibilities.

It is through consciousness that we translate energy waves into tangible experiences.
Rupert Sheldrake's theory of morphic resonance suggests the existence of a morphogenetic field connecting all beings and forms of life. This field acts as a cosmic library storing information and experiences. When a human has an experience or gains knowledge, this morphogenetic field updates, allowing others more access to the same information.
While Carl Jung introduced the concept of the Collective Unconscious, suggesting shared elements in the psyche of all people, I, myself, prefer the philosophical context of a Collective Mind—where we would be unified under a Higher Consciousness.

Remember, science and spirituality are intertwined in the tapestry of reality—it's a fusion for your evolution and transformation. We'll continue navigating the depths of the science of consciousness, simultaneously exploring the depths of our being. We are all the navigators of this ocean of possibilities, and our minds are the compasses guiding us to uncharted lands—where everything is possible and all becomes reality.

18

Quantum Law

Navigating the Realm of Possibilities

"Quantum law not only responds to what we see; it responds to the vibrations we emit"

In the realm of possibilities, quantum law orchestrates the overture of creation. It's the universal plane conducting the symphony of events, shaping our reality based on the vibrations of our thoughts and emotions. It's like a tenor singing an aria with a soprano—a synchronized melody with vibrations and coloratura—though invisible; they are emitted and materialize through their voices.

Here's where the magic happens: Quantum law responds not only to what we see but to the vibrations we emit. Like the music we hear live or wirelessly through modulated frequencies.

This metaphor is a familiar experience for me—when my daughter Lola sings my favorite opera arias and other songs, and I enjoy the resonant vibrations of my son Nick's guitars, and my niece Johanna delights me with her piano—this reflects that deep connection in those precious moments harmonizing melodies full of affection. It became a living manifestation of how synchronized energies magically blend and transcend the barriers of time and space.
This beautiful musical example illustrates the magic of the cosmic connection that surrounds and envelops us in an eternal embrace with a deep resonance of kindred souls in a celebration of harmony across generations.

This law is not constrained by the limitations of time and space; instead, it operates beyond our conventional understanding of cause and effect. The fundamental principle of quantum law is that energy attracts similar energy. It means the frequencies we send into the field match and attract corresponding frequencies. Like tuning forks of the same frequency resonate when one is struck, our thoughts and emotions connect with events and circumstances that mirror their energy.
Think of it as a dance floor where partners gravitate toward each other in perfect synchrony. When our energy aligns with the frequency of a potential reality, we create a magnetic pull that draws that reality into our experience. That's why our emotional state is vital; it guides us toward realities that align with our vibrations.

Quantum law thrives on possibility. It reminds us that the universe is a field of infinite potential, with countless paths awaiting our exploration. The moment we focus our thoughts and feelings on a particular outcome, we send a signal to the universe, setting in motion a series of events that lead us toward that outcome.

So, how does quantum law navigate the vast expanse of potential realities? The answer lies in our intention. We direct our energy toward a specific destination when we infuse our intention with clarity, emotion, and purpose. It's like giving the cosmos a precise address to deliver our desires.

Consider quantum law as a cosmic postal service, delivering experience packages to your door. The contents of these packages are shaped by the energy you've invested in your intentions. Whether love, success, healing, or abundance, quantum law responds to your intentions impeccably.

Embracing quantum law requires an open heart and an expansive mind. It's about recognizing that the cosmos is not a rigid structure but a fluid and receptive field. It's about understanding that every thought and emotion we emit is a stroke on the canvas of creation.

As co-creators of our reality, we have the privilege and responsibility to wield the brush of intention with care and wisdom. By harnessing the power of quantum law, we align with the orchestration of the cosmos. We become conscious participants in the grand dance of existence, contributing our unique colors to the ever-evolving masterpiece.

19

The Law of Thought Vibration

Tuning into Your Desires

"The law of vibration is the score that guides your interpretation, ensuring that the notes you play are the same ones returned in the echo of your reality"

In the vast theater of life, the Law of Thought Vibration, widely known as the Law of Attraction, is one of the main acts. Here, thoughts take center stage, unveiling the mysterious Laws of Vibration and Attraction. This law reminds us that we are emotional magnets, drawing towards us experiences and circumstances that resonate with our inner energy. Every thought, every emotion, every vibration we emit is like a signal sent to the cosmos, dictating what we will manifest in our reality.

Imagine being the conductor of the cosmic orchestra, directing the melody of your life. The thoughts and emotions you tune into are the notes composing your song. The Law of Vibration is the sheet music guiding your performance, ensuring the notes you play are the ones echoed back in reality around you.

This law operates based on resonance. We attract what we vibrate. If our vibrations are filled with gratitude, love, and joy, we attract experiences and people reflecting those emotions. On the other hand, if our vibrations are loaded with fear, doubt, and negativity, we attract situations and individuals corresponding to that emotional state. I call it the "Echo Law"—what we emit comes back to us; you are your mirror, and your emotional state will be reflected in your surroundings.

The process of the Law of Thought Vibration is simple yet profound. It begins with the seed of a thought. This thought generates an emotion, which, in turn, generates a vibration. This vibration acts as a signal the universe picks up and reflects into our reality. It's like sending a message to the universe and receiving a response as an experience.

Here's the secret: the key is not just thinking about what we want but feeling it with our whole being. Emotion is the catalyst that accelerates materialization. When we feel strong and positive emotions while thinking about what we desire, we align our energy with that reality. It creates a resonance that will attract what we want towards us.

It's crucial to remember that the Law of Thought Vibration doesn't judge if our thoughts are positive or negative. It simply reflects the energy we emit. If we focus on what we don't want, our universe will respond to that energy and deliver more of the same. If we focus on what we desire and feel it passionately, the universe will respond to that energy with matching experiences.

Sometimes, the Law of Thought Vibration may seem magical. But, it's a universal principle operating constantly in our lives.

As co-creators of our reality, we have the power to decide what kind of energy we want to emit and, consequently, what kind of experiences we want to attract.

Remember, you are the master of your energy. You have the power to tune your thoughts and emotions to your deepest desires. In doing so, you are tuning your cosmic instrument and creating a symphony of experiences that will resonate with the melody of your heart.

20

The Magic of Gratitude and Reception

"When we cultivate gratitude, we open the doors to the magic of receiving"

What is gratitude? Gratitude is a magical force that transforms our perspective and connects our hearts with the universe's abundance. When we cultivate gratitude, we open the doors to the magic of receiving. In this chapter, we'll explore the duet between gratitude and reception, discovering how this symphony can elevate our lives and enable us to co-create with the cosmos.

The Dance of Gratitude

At this stage of life, gratitude is the music guiding our dance. It's a sincere expression of appreciation for all that we are and have. When we move to the rhythm of gratitude, we create a magnetic field that attracts more blessings to our experience. From sunrise to sunset, we can find reasons to be thankful, thereby elevating our vibration and allowing us to flow in harmony with the universe.

Transforming Challenges into Opportunities
Gratitude is about appreciating what goes well but also about finding the light in the midst of darkness. When we face challenges, we can shift our perspective and look for the lessons they offer. In every adversity and obstacle, there is an opportunity for growth. By transforming our challenges into opportunities, we become alchemists of our reality and dance with gratitude even in difficult moments.

The Influence of Gratitude on Health and Well-being
Our body and mind are intimately connected, and gratitude profoundly impacts both. The regular practice of gratitude has been scientifically linked to stress reduction, mood improvement, and a more robust immune system. Opening our hearts to gratitude allows a healing current to flow, nurturing our overall well-being.

Gratitude as a Manifestation Tool
Gratitude is a key that unlocks the door of manifestation. When we thank for what we have before it happens, we send a compelling signal to the universe indicating our readiness to receive more. By expressing gratitude for our future blessings, we set the stage for their arrival. Gra-

titude is not just an attitude but also a powerful tool of co-creation.

Summing Up:
The Symphony of Gratitude and Reception
In life's score, gratitude and reception are notes creating a beautiful symphony. By living with gratitude and allowing ourselves to receive with an open heart, we become active participants in the cosmos' choreography. As we dance with appreciation, we harmonize our lives with the abundance and joy always around us.

21

The Science of Consciousness and Quantum Physics

"Realizing that we are active participants in creating reality, we reclaim a power we may have forgotten"

In the beautiful tapestry of reality, consciousness, and quantum physics waltz together in a mysterious and captivating dance. Imagine consciousness as that spark of self-awareness within us, the maestro orchestrating our experiences. Now, picture quantum physics as the bold explorer, delving into the subatomic realms, offering a revolutionary canvas of reality.

Consciousness isn't a passive observer in life's theater—it's a dynamic force engaging with the world around us. Science is catching up with ancient wisdom, hinting that mind and matter share an intricate connection.

Quantum physics flips our understanding upside down. Subatomic particles, in their minuscule realm, can exist in multiple states simultaneously, and they dance in tandem through a mystical link called "quantum entanglement."
Yes, these revelations challenge our traditional grasp of reality. The fascinating part is that consciousness plays a role in this quantum reality. Experiments show that observing subatomic particles influences their behavior. Our focused attention has this magical ability to touch the subatomic world and, consequently, the world we see and feel daily.

This discovery implies a profound connection between mind and matter. Our consciousness and intention hold the potential to shape reality in ways that one once thought impossible. Realizing that we're active participants in creating reality gives us back a power we might have forgotten.
The science of consciousness and quantum physics signal us to expand our horizons and question our limiting beliefs. They invite us to embrace the idea that we're not mere spectators but co-creators of our world. As we embark on this exploration, we open ourselves to new possibilities and discover a universe overflowing us with infinite potential.

Remember, each thought and emotion you hold sends a signal to the universe. The universe, in its quantum dance, responds to these signals. Understanding the profound connection between consciousness and reality is like unlocking an inner power that can transform not only our lives but the entire world we inhabit.

22

The Journey to Self-Realization

"Self-realization is an act of self-love. It is the commitment to honor our deepest needs, dreams, and desires"

In life's grand journey, the pursuit of self-realization is like a radiant beacon guiding us through the tumultuous waves of existence. It's that deep yearning to uncover our most authentic selves, an ongoing adventure of self-discovery and growth.

Self-realization isn't just a destination; it's an ever-unfolding path of peeling away layers of societal expectations and personal conditioning. Picture it as a journey within, where you gradually unveil the unique essence dwelling in your core.

As you navigate this path, you encounter challenges and opportunities, each becoming a stepping stone for your growth. Whether bathed in joy or facing difficulty, every experience is a chance to learn more about yourself and discern your purpose in life.

Self-realization is an act of profound self-love. It's a commitment to honor your needs, dreams, and deepest desires, freeing yourself from the demands you might impose and fully embracing your authenticity.

On this journey, self-compassion becomes a cherished companion. Treating yourself with kindness and gentleness forms a strong connection with your inner self. You learn to listen to your inner voices and trust your intuition, creating a harmonious relationship within us.

Self-realization is also about seeking meaning and purpose. It encourages you to explore your unique passions and talents, utilizing them to impact the world positively. Aligning your actions with your deepest values brings a sense of fulfillment and wholeness.

This path may be challenging, but it's profoundly rewarding. Every step brings you closer to your essence, fostering a deeper connection with yourself and the universe.

Call to mind: self-realization is a personal journey—yet it's a reminder of your interconnectedness with all living beings. As you ascend and evolve, you inspire others to do the same, creating a more conscious and loving world.

At every turn on this path, know you are worthy of love, happiness, and success. You're a unique manifestation of the universe's creative energy, and your journey of self-realization is a precious gift you can offer to yourself.

23

The Path of Self-Transcendence

"Self-transcendence is the expansion of our being beyond the confines of our ego"
"By freeing ourselves from resistance and inflexibility, we allow the magic of life to unfold before us"

In the quest for a deeper purpose, the journey of self-transcendence unfolds like a bright trail stretching toward the horizon. It's a venture that takes us beyond the borders of ourselves and weaves our essence with the vastness of the cosmos.

Self-transcendence means stretching our existence beyond the edges of our ego, acknowledging that we are threads in a larger tapestry, interwoven with all beings and life itself. On this path, recognizing that our actions ripple through the very fabric of reality, we become conscious contributors to the co-creation of the world.

To transcend ourselves, we must release the grip of control and surrender to the wisdom of the cosmos. It's an act of trust, believing that the natural flow of life will guide us where we need to go. As we shed resistance, the magic of life unfolds before us.

One of the most beautiful aspects of self-transcendence is experiencing universal compassion. Rising above selfish concerns, we see the interconnectedness of all life forms, cultivating unconditional love for every being. Authenticity becomes our compass on this journey, freeing us from self-assigned masks and roles and allowing our true selves to shine and contribute uniquely to the world's well-being.

Self-Transcendence signals us to explore the essence of reality, pushing us to question who we are beyond labels and roles. In this exploration of our inner selves, we discover that we are more than our thoughts, emotions, and experiences.

This journey also leads us to humility and gratitude, recognizing that we are always learning and growing.

Every challenge and every triumph propels us forward on this path of expansion and evolution.

In embracing the unity and diversity woven into the fabric of existence, we dissolve the illusion of separation.

24

The Dance of Co-Creation

"Trust in co-creation is nurturing by faith that everything happens at the perfect time and place"

In the vast canvas of existence, we, as life's artists, possess the incredible ability to co-create our reality.
Co-creation is a dance, a dialogue between our intentions and the universe's response, an intricate partnership between our inner selves and life's flow.

Picture yourself as a sculptor, molding your creation with a clear vision and focused intention. Feel the excitement of living that reality as if it's already yours. Yet, co-creation isn't confined to the realm of thought. It's about infusing your vision and intention into the depths of your being, where the magic unfolds as you align your vision with positive, vibrant emotions.

The next step involves releasing attachments to the 'hows' and 'whens.' Instead of micromanaging the details, trust in the universe's intelligence. This isn't passivity; it's active participation in the materialization process.

Trust in co-creation thrives on faith, believing everything unfolds at the perfect time and place. Trusting that the universe conspires in your favor opens you to receiving what you need to bring your vision to life.

Gratitude is an essential companion on this journey, magnifying co-creation energy and attracting more blessings. Remember, you are an energetic magnet, drawing experiences in harmony with your vibration. Conscious co-creation empowers you to adjust and elevate your vibration through thoughts, emotions, and actions. In the dance of co-creation, receptivity is crucial—pay attention to signs, synchronicities, and opportunities. Sometimes, what seems coincidental is a universe's gift supporting your journey.

As you navigate your co-creation journey, keep your vision clear, your heart open, and your mind receptive. You are an active collaborator in the cosmos, an artist of reality working hand in hand with the universe to breathe life into your dreams.

25

The Creation of a New Reality

"Conscious creation is a dynamic dance between our vision and cosmic intelligence"

Picture life as this awe-inspiring tapestry where our intentions are like threads weaving its intricate design. Every thought and emotion we hold is a strand, contributing to the unfolding pattern of our destiny. But how do we consciously harness this creative power to sculpt our lives as we dream?

The answer lies in alignment—syncing our mind, emotions, and energy with what we want to bring into existence. When our thoughts harmonize with our goals, we create a magnetic force, pulling in circumstances and opportunities that resonate with our vision.

Imagine having an inner compass guiding you toward your aspirations. You activate this internal compass when you adjust your mental and emotional focus to vibe with your desires. It steers you towards decisions and actions aligned with your intentions, inching you closer to your envisioned future.

Consistency is crucial here. When we maintain coherence between our thoughts, feelings, and actions, we send the universe a clear message: "I'm ready to receive this into my life." The universe responds in kind to the vibes we emit.
But conscious creation is more than just wishing and waiting; it demands action. We must be ready to take steps toward our goals, even when the whole picture isn't clear. Action acts as the bridge connecting our inner world with the external one.
Trust is the linchpin. Trust that you're on the right path, even when the details are fuzzy. Trust that the universe has your back every step of the way. Trust that you deserve the blessings you're bringing into your life. This trust nurtures the seed of your creation, allowing it to bloom to its full potential.

Conscious creation also means letting go of control. Clinging too tightly to a specific idea can limit the countless ways the cosmos might surprise us. By releasing control and allowing things to flow, we make space for the universe to unfold its magical and surprising dance.
Ultimately, *"conscious creation is a dynamic dance between our vision and cosmic intelligence."*

It's a partnership between our focused minds and the rhythm of life. As we step into this dance, we discover that we are co-creators of our reality, moving in harmony with the cosmos.

26

Embracing Inner Power

"We are more powerful than we often realize, and our ability to create and shape our reality is limitless"

At the core of our being lies a wellspring of untapped potential, eagerly waiting to be tapped into and expressed. We're far more potent than we often give ourselves credit for, and our capacity to mold and shape our reality knows no bounds.

The key to unlocking this power lies in recognizing and fully embracing our true nature. We're not isolated entities —we're an integral part of the grand tapestry of the universe. Much like a wave is an inseparable part of the ocean— we are threads in the cosmic fabric of existence.

When we connect with this awareness—we tap into a force that transcends time and space constraints. We become co-creators with the universe—sculpting our reality through our thoughts, emotions, and intentions. Our consciousness becomes the bridge that connects the inner and outer worlds.

This power isn't an external force; it's an internal flame burning brightly within us. The fire of our desires, the energy of our dreams, and the driving force propels us forward.

Aligning our thoughts and emotions with our deepest desires transforms us into conduits for materializing those desires.
Yet, this process necessitates a shift in mindset. We must shed limiting beliefs and doubts that have held us captive. Cultivating self-awareness and tuning into our inner dialogue becomes paramount. In doing so, we can reprogram our thoughts and beliefs to align with our loftiest potential. Meditation and mindfulness practices emerge as invaluable tools on this transformative journey. They help silence the external noise, creating a space for inner stillness. In this sanctuary, we can listen to the whispers of our intuition and tap into the wellspring of creativity within.

By embracing our inner power, we step into a realm of empowerment. We recognize that we are not mere victims of circumstances but architects of our destiny. We understand that our thoughts and emotions are the building blocks of the reality we construct.

This journey of Self-Mastery and Self-Discovery is a continuing odyssey—it demands patience, dedication, and a readiness to embrace the unknown. Yet, as we delve into the recesses of our consciousness—we unlock the doors to our true potential and unearth the enchantment within us.

27

The Path to Mastery

"As we progress on this path, we become alchemists of our reality"

Mastery isn't just about being really good at something; it's a journey, a commitment to growth that spans a lifetime. It's like becoming an artist of your own existence.

Think of it as more than mastering external skills—it's an internal quest. It's about diving deep into who you are at your core and understanding how you weave into the grand tapestry of the universe. It's like unlocking the ancient wisdom embedded within you.

But mastery is no walk in the park. It's a path that demands courage. You're not just overcoming obstacles but turning challenges into stepping stones for growth.

Masters don't shy away from failure; they embrace it as another lesson on the road to success.

Authenticity is the North Star on this journey. It's about shedding the layers that aren't truly you and standing in your genuine self. No more seeking approval; instead, it's about trusting your gut and the wisdom deep within.

The journey to mastery isn't a solo trip. As you expand and evolve, you become a guide for others, sharing the wisdom you've gained. It's like being a lighthouse, helping others navigate their seas.

Sure, it's tough, but the rewards are beyond measure. Living in sync with the universe, shaping your destiny consciously—you're not just a participant; you're a co-creator, leaving an everlasting mark.

And remember, it's not a destination but a daily practice. Every day unfolds new lessons, offering chances to learn, grow, and evolve.

28

Living in Harmony

"When you are in harmony, you will notice that you naturally attract people, situations, and opportunities that align with your energy"

Living in harmony is a lot like dancing to the beat of your own soul. It's not about being flawless but about embracing your true self. Imagine life as a flowing river, and you're in sync with its rhythm.
It all starts with self-awareness. Take a moment, connect with your inner self, and ponder what truly lights your fire. Let that understanding guide your decisions, aligning them with your authentic self.

When you're in harmony, it's like a cosmic magnetism. People, opportunities, and situations naturally gravitate towards you. It's not luck; it's your vibe attracting your tribe. But harmony is a daily gig. It's not a one-time decision but a continuous effort. Regularly check in with yourself, ensuring your thoughts and actions vibe with your true self. Sometimes, it means making tough calls that honor your authenticity.

Living in harmony involves decluttering. Let go of what no longer serves you—old beliefs, habits, relationships—creating space for new energies to flow into your life.
And this harmony extends to your goals and dreams. When your intentions align with your true self, they become an extension of who you are. It's like the universe nods in agreement.

Remember, it's not about being flawless but about being authentic. Embrace your quirks, vulnerabilities, and strengths. When you're in harmony, you emit an energy that draws others in, inspiring them to do the same.

29

Quantum Law
Your Cosmic Co-Creator

*"Align your frequency with your desires and let the
quantum law work magic"*

In the enchanting tapestry of existence, you're a unique thread intricately woven into the fabric of the universe. Quantum law directs this cosmic symphony, where your intentions and emotions resonate to shape the reality(,) you experience.

Picture quantum law as the ultimate law of attraction, surpassing any wish-granting mechanism. It responds not just to your conscious desires but also to the energy of your emotions and thoughts. It's like the universe decoding the codes of your heart and mind to orchestrate the dance of creation.

This law is the master of paradoxes. It thrives in uncertainty and ambiguity, responding to the dual nature of waves and particles. It invites you to embrace the dance between potentiality and actualization. In this dance — you're both the choreographer and the dancer, co-creating every step of the journey.

Quantum law doesn't operate in isolation; it harmonizes with other universal laws, weaving an intricate web of principles governing the cosmos. As you navigate life, remember you're an observer and a participant in this cosmic ballet. Your thoughts, emotions, and intentions influence the patterns woven into the fabric of reality.

So, how can you harness the power of quantum law in your favor? Start with mindful awareness and thoughtful intention. You're not a mere accidental spectator in this universe; you're a conscious co-creator. Your thoughts and emotions are like seeds planted in the fertile soil of the cosmos, ready to sprout into tangible experiences.

But this power comes with responsibility. As you handle Quantum Law, remember the energy you emit ripples through the cosmos and returns to you in kind. Your intentions and emotions shape the reality you experience, so ensure they reflect the world you want to see.

Quantum law isn't just an abstract concept; it's a lived experience. Embrace the interplay of energies, thoughts, and emotions. Align your frequency with your desires and let quantum law do its magic. Open your mind to synchronicities, quantum surprises, and serendipitous events that will come your way.

As you plunge into the realm of quantum law, remember you're not alone. The universe conspires to co-create with you. Trust the infinite possibilities laid out before you. Feel the vibrations of the cosmos resonating within you. You are the cosmic co-creator, and quantum law is your partner in materialization.

30

The Exploration of Self

"The exploration of the self is an invitation to authenticity. It encourages you to embrace all aspects of your being, even those that may seem uncomfortable or contradictory. By recognizing and accepting all of your parts, you free yourself from the need to hide or suppress your true essence"

Diving into exploring self is like venturing into a vast ocean of self-awareness. It's a journey taking you to the depths of your own mind, emotions, and essence. As you embark on this path, you discover hidden layers of yourself waiting to be unveiled.

Self-exploration involves observing your thoughts and emotions from an impartial perspective. You become an observer of your own mind, neither judging nor identifying with every thought that arises. This practice allows you to understand your rooted thought patterns and emotions. In this journey, you also discover that you are much more than your thoughts and emotions. Behind the active mind, there's a space of silence and stillness. In that space, you connect with a sense of calm and peace that is always present, even amidst external chaos.

The exploration of self leads you to question your ingrained beliefs and the stories you tell yourself. It encourages you to examine your motivations and delve deep into the deeper layers of your being; you encounter aspects of yourself that you may have been avoiding or unaware of.

This journey can also unearth repressed or forgotten emotions. Though challenging, it's essential to allow yourself to feel and heal these emotions. By facing and releasing what you've been holding onto, you create space for greater mental and emotional clarity.

The exploration of self is an invitation to authenticity — it urges you to embrace all aspects of your being — even those that might seem uncomfortable or contradictory. By recognizing and accepting all parts of yourself, you free yourself from the need to hide or suppress your true essence.

This journey is continuous and never-ending. As you grow and evolve, the layers of your being keep unfolding. Exploring the self empowers you to live from a place of greater authenticity, understanding, and acceptance. It enables you to live a life aligned with your true self and contribute uniquely to the world around you.

31

Unity in Diversity

Weaving Connections in the Cosmos

"We open the door to compassion and empathy by embracing diversity in all its forms"

In this cosmic existence, diversity is one of the most vibrant and essential threads. The universe is woven with various forms, energies, and expressions from distant galaxies to humans on Earth. Though it may seem we are separate, we are, in reality, connected at a profound level of unity.

Science tells us that all elements in the universe originated in stars–we are literally stardust. The atoms composing our bodies, the Earth beneath our feet, and the air we breathe were forged in the fiery core of stars in spectacular explosions. In this sense, we all share a common cosmic heritage.

Biology reveals that every form of life on Earth shares a genetic foundation. Our biological structures are intertwined in a web of interdependent life from plants to animals. Our ecosystems are complex relationships of symbiosis and balance, where each being plays a crucial role in the health of the whole.

Quantum physics speaks of instant connection between entangled particles, no matter how far apart they are in space. It suggests that, at a fundamental level, the concept of distance might be an illusion in the quantum fabric of reality. In this cosmic dance, we are bound by invisible threads that transcend space and time.
Worldwide spiritual traditions also speak of unity in diversity. From the Eastern philosophy of "Tao" to the indigenous concept of the "web of life," ancient teachings remind us that we are all part of an interconnected whole. The illusion of separation is merely an illusion.

In our journey of self-exploration and growth, we can remember this underlying unity. We open the door to compassion and empathy by embracing diversity in all its forms. Recognizing our connection to everything, we can begin to care for ourselves but also for others and the planet we share.
So, as we navigate the cosmic dance of life, let's remember that while each of us is unique and special, we are all part of one story.

Diversity is our strength, and unity is our essence. In this dance, we are all fellow travelers exploring the vast landscape of possibilities on the universe's canvas.

32

Free Will and Destiny

"Each choice and thought we have are like pieces of a puzzle that fit into the broader picture of our destiny"

In the flow of life, we encounter the dilemma of free will, that gift the universe bestows upon us to make conscious decisions and choices. The rudder allows us to steer the course of our lives. Every day, we are surrounded by countless options, from the most trivial to those that define our future. Free will represents our ability to influence that destiny, to be the architects of our own reality.

We often wonder if our choices matter in a universe where larger forces are at play. But, as we'll explore in this chapter, every choice and every thought we have is like pieces of a puzzle fitting into the broader picture of our destiny. Through our actions and choices, we wield our power to influence that destiny, shape it, and give it meaning.

We'll delve into how our everyday actions and personal decisions reflect our innate ability to co-create the destiny we forge—exploring how free will is not just a belief but a living force that propels us through life.

In this journey, we uncover how our conscious choices act as seeds we plant in the garden of our destiny and how these seeds germinate and bloom the realities we create ourselves. The next step is to dive into the thread of destiny, where we'll explore how events that may seem random at first glance fit into a larger pattern. We'll also examine how destiny can manifest through serendipities and epiphanies, those moments of sudden clarity illuminating our minds.

The Thread of Destiny:

Destiny is often associated with a force beyond our control. We are analyzing how seemingly random events can fit into a larger pattern and how destiny can materialize through serendipities and epiphanies—those moments of sudden clarity illuminating our minds. These mysterious and often astonishing events are signals from the universe, reminding us that we are part of something much greater and significant.

At this point in the journey, we plunge into the intriguing dichotomy of predetermined destiny and free will. At first glance, these concepts may seem in conflict, like two streams of water colliding. Destiny is often associated with a force beyond our control, with events and experiences that seem written in the stars, immutable and predetermined.

However, as we explore more deeply, we discover that destiny is not a chain that binds us but rather a thread that intertwines all the choices and experiences of our lives. Our personal choices, our free will, are like hands weaving that thread of destiny, shaping it and giving it meaning as we move forward.

It's as if each choice and thought is a link in an infinite chain of possibilities. Every decision we make takes us down a particular path, but there are still multiple trails within that path. It's our free will that determines which path we choose to follow.

This balance between destiny and free will may seem confusing initially. Still, as we expand our awareness and explore these ideas, we realize that we are ultimately co-creators of our destiny.

We are not puppets in the hands of a predetermined destiny; we are the directors of our masterpieces. Or, as some theories suggest, we are part of a vast cosmic matrix, and the universal creative mind guides us like characters in a virtual game. In this universe filled with possibilities, my perspective remains neutral, leaving room for curiosity and more profound investigation of these fascinating theories and forming my own conclusions as I progress in this journey of self-discovery.

We continue to explore conscious creation under the tools we possess, bringing to life a reality that each of us can only choose. I profoundly believe in those serendipities and epiphanies, which I call 'my synchronicities, signs, and evidence.' I observe how they manifest extraordinarily, flowing and reminding me that I have the power to co-create and tune into the correct vibrational frequency to bring forth the reality I desire.

Examples of Free Will vs. Destiny:
In this section, we will immerse ourselves in concrete examples to illustrate how our decisions and choices can collide or harmonize with what seems to be our predetermined destiny.

> **Career Journey:** Imagine someone who has dreamed of being a doctor since *childhood. This ambition may result from their family environment or simply an inner calling. They choose to study medicine and dedicate years to education and training. As their career progresses, they encounter unexpected opportunities and make decisions that eventually lead them to specialize in a particular medical branch. Was their choice to become a doctor a manifestation of their free will, or was their destiny linked to that career from the beginning?*

> ***Encounters and Friendships:** Throughout life, we meet many people. Some of these connections are coincidences, while others seem destined. An unexpected encounter at a social event may lead to a lasting friendship. On the other hand, a relationship that seemed destined may*

crumble due to personal choices. How can we discern when destiny guides our relationships and when our free will comes into play?

Discerning between free will and destiny, where perception can be subjective and largely dependent on our beliefs and each person's philosophy, some may believe that everything is predestined. In contrast, others believe in a higher degree of free will.
We need to find that balance between "destiny and free will" that will resonate with each of us and allow for conscious decision-making. Some of us have experienced that intuitive feeling or precognition and reflect that everything has happened for a reason—as an element of destiny or a mission we have to fulfill—as well as a combination of both, leaning towards one or the other perspective. When everything aligns smoothly and effortlessly, that feeling can be interpreted as if you're in tune with your destiny or mission—at a moment when things seem to fit perfectly, which can strengthen the belief in a certain degree of destiny or purpose in life.

It's a complex, profound, and fascinating subject that has been the cause of debates in philosophy and spirituality for centuries.

33

Serendipities and Epiphanies

"Amid serendipity and epiphanies, we discover that the universe speaks to us in whispers—guiding our steps toward a destiny we are co-creating"

Serendipities and epiphanies are two phenomena that often take people by surprise but can profoundly impact their lives. These experiences, although different in nature, share the quality of opening new doors and offering a fresh view of the world.

Serendipities are those magical moments in which something valuable or significant is revealed when we least expect it. Often, these experiences occur while we are busy looking for something completely different. A classic example is the discovery of penicillin by the scientist Alexander Fleming, who noticed mold growth on his petri dish while investigating bacteria. Serendipities remind us that the world is a place full of surprises and that sometimes the answers we look for can be found in the least thought-out places.

Epiphanies, however, are like flashes of understanding that suddenly illuminate our minds. These moments of clarity can change the way we see the world and give us a new perspective on important issues. Another classic example is the famous apple that fell on Isaac Newton's head, which led him to understand the law of gravity. But the epiphanies are not exclusive to geniuses like Newton; we can all experience moments of deep understanding that inspire and transform us.

Many years ago, during a trip to Spain, I was under an olive tree enjoying its shade with my children and my little niece Johanna. At one point, an olive fell on my head. It may sound trivial, but that little incident became a moment of deep understanding for me. It was as if the universe itself had thrown that olive to remind me of the importance of the unexpected. That incident marked the beginning of my journey towards a greater understanding of the mind, energy, and creativity—and yes, I understood even more what happened to the great alchemist and physicist Isaac Newton.

In the same way, we all have our own experiences of serendipities and epiphanies that influence our life and work.

Sharing these experiences connects us on a deeper level, and I love to give a personal touch to the work.

My experience with that olive was the starting point of a fascinating exploration in my life. I kept that little olive as a memory, a reminder of the mystery behind that seemingly casual event. It led me to wonder what meaning it could have if I had any, and what lessons I could draw from it. My curiosity prompted me to investigate more about olives and their importance in Spanish culture. That's when I discovered more about the richness of Spanish extra virgin olive oil, which contains centuries of tradition and quality. But what surprised me even more was to find out that my great-grandparents, noble landowners, had been olive growers and produced oils, part of the story I didn't know. The connection between my personal history and this family tradition was a moment of profound epiphany, which I had to reach because I had the mission of finding my family's legacy.

This discovery became one of the guiding threads of my search for understanding. It represented a connection with my family roots and symbolized the power of serendipity in our lives and how seemingly casual events can lead us to unexpected and meaningful paths. On my magical journey, they have been one after another, which still seems unreal to me —I have wonderful people by my side who accompany me and whom I love deeply.
So, as you can see, my own experience with an olive triggered a series of events that changed the course of my life,

and thanks to all this, I now have the legacy of my family that I will leave to the new generations.

Amid serendipities and epiphanies, we discover that the universe speaks to us in whispers—guiding our steps toward a destiny we are co-creating.

Promoting the Role of Serendipities and Epiphanies

> *How you can promote serendipities in your life:* The importance of curiosity, openness to new experiences, and the willingness to deviate from routine.
>
> *Curiosity awakens:* Be open to the possibility that something surprising or unusual may happen at any time. Encouraging curiosity in your daily life allows you to notice patterns or connections that would go unnoticed.
>
> *Observing with an open mind:* Practicing conscious observation helps you to be more in tune with your environment. This involves seeing, hearing, smelling, and feeling what surrounds you. By observing with an open mind, you can capture signals or clues that others might overlook.
>
> *Clarity and transformation:* Serendipities often occur in moments of reflection or when you look for answers. Mental clarity and willingness to explore new perspectives can lead to surprising discoveries and transformative changes.

Unexpected connections: *Pay attention to the connections that develop between seemingly unrelated events. Sometimes, serendipity manifests when you realize how two seemingly different events, people, or ideas connect meaningfully.*

Emotional impact: *Serendipities are usually accompanied by a strong emotional response. It can be a feeling of astonishment, joy, inspiration, or even a spark of creativity. Paying attention to your emotions will help you recognize when you are experiencing serendipity.*

Synchronicities: *Synchronicities are significant events that are related in a non-causal way. When you find repeated patterns or pay attention to connections between events in your life since they could be serendipities in action.*

Sense of purpose: *Serendipities often seem to align with your personal goals or desires. It could be a sign of serendipity if you find yourself in situations that bring you closer to your goals unexpectedly. Acute Intuition: Trust your intuition and those moments when you feel an "impulse" to follow a path or make a particular decision. Sometimes, intuition can indicate that a serendipity is about to occur.*

Sharp intuition: *Trust your intuition and those moments when you feel an 'urge' to follow a path or make a* *particular decision. Sometimes, intuition can hint that a serendipity is about to occur.*

Surprising coincidence: *Pay attention to the surprising coincidences. Sometimes, those strange coincidences can be an invitation to explore further.*

Learn from surprises: *Finally, keep a learning mindset. Each serendipity is an opportunity to learn something new, even if, at that moment, you do not fully understand its meaning.*

The role of epiphanies in creativity: *Explores how epiphanies often play a crucial role in creativity and problem-solving.*

Recognizing the Epiphanies

The Epiphanies are like flashes of understanding that suddenly illuminate our minds. These experiences may seem unpredictable, like serendipities, but their distinctive features make them unique. Here are some ways to recognize them:

Instantaneous clarity: *An epiphany often feels like a sudden burst of clarity. Suddenly, you understand something that previously seemed confusing or disconcerting to you. This feeling of clarity can be so powerful that it can instantly change your perspective.*

Connection of ideas: *Epiphanies often involve the connection of apparently unrelated ideas. You may have been thinking about a problem for a long time, and suddenly, a connection forms in your mind, revealing a solution or a new understanding.*

The feeling of depth: *Epiphanies tend to go beyond a simple observation or discovery. They can get to the root of a problem or provide a deep insight that changes how you see a situation.*

Lasting impact: *Epiphanies often have a lasting impact on your life. They are not just fleeting moments of clarity; they can change the way you act, make decisions, and relate to the world around you.*

Feeling of inspiration: *Epiphanies are often accompanied by a feeling of inspiration and emotion. They can fill you with energy and motivation to move forward.*

Epiphanies as Catalysts for Creativity

Epiphanies play a crucial role in the world of creativity. They are those magical moments in which the mind suddenly lights up, revealing new perspectives, innovative ideas or creative solutions to previously enigmatic problems. This spark of illumination is not only exciting but also a driving force behind human creativity.

The creative awakening: *Epiphanies are like flashes of inspiration that break into our lives, often when we least expect it. They can happen while we shower, walk in the park, or even at night. These moments of clarity are like a gift from the cosmos, revealing hidden connections and creative opportunities.*

Lateral thinking: *Most of us are accustomed to thinking in a linear and structured way. However, epiphanies often lead us to think "outside the box." It is as if a new path was opened before us, defying the previously established limitations. This is essential for creativity since it breaks with conventions and allows new forms of expression.*

The "Eureka" moment: *Throughout history, inventors, artists and scientists have experienced the "eureka" moment, an expression of joy when an epiphany leads them to a revolutionary solution. This type of discovery is not only exciting for the individual but also has the potential to transform entire industries or change the way we see the world.*

Connection of points: *Epiphanies are often experienced as the connection of points that previously seemed scattered. A complex problem can be suddenly simplified when we see the relationship between different ideas or concepts. This reinforces the idea that creativity is not only about trying to generate new ideas, but also about recognizing unexpected connections.*

A dance between the conscious and the subconscious: The epiphanies also illustrate the fascinating interaction between the conscious mind and the subconscious. Often, our minds work in the background, processing information unconsciously until, in a moment of epiphany, that information rises to consciousness. This process is a testimony to the depth and scope of our mind.

In short, epiphanies catalyze creativity by unlocking new perspectives and solutions. They are potent reminders that the human mind can find beauty in surprise and innovation in the unexpected. Throughout history, these epiphanies have shaped our world and continue to be sources of inspiration and transformation.

The Role of Epiphanies in Creativity

On a deeper level, epiphanies are like seeds that, when planted in the fertile mind, can grow and give rise to unbridled creativity.

Here are some ways in which epiphanies play a crucial role in creativity:

Sudden inspiration: Epiphanies can be instant sources of inspiration. In one moment, you may feel trapped in an idea or blocked in your creativity; in the next, an epiphany shows you a completely new path. This can be *especially useful when facing a creative or artistic project and needing a fresh twist.*

Solving creative blocks: *Creative blocks are common challenges for artists and creators. Epiphanies have the power to dissolve these blockages by presenting surprising and unconventional solutions. They show you that there are many ways to address a problem, and often, the answer is in an unexpected place.*

Innovation and business creativity: *In the business world, epiphanies are the engine of innovation. Many successful companies have originated from an innovative idea that was generated due to an epiphany. These moments of clarity can change the trajectory of a company and give rise to revolutionary products and services.*

Unexpected connections: *Epiphanies are also experts in making unexpected connections. They can take you from a seemingly isolated idea to a network of related concepts. This ability to connect seemingly scattered points is fundamental to creativity since those connections are often where true originality resides.*

Revelation of potential: *Epiphanies not only reveal new ideas but also reveal the latent potential in existing ideas. They can show how an idea you consider familiar transforms something extraordinary. This encourages* *a creative mindset by exploring family concepts from unexplored angles.*

The adventure of creativity: *Epiphanies are often experienced as exciting adventures of the mind. They are like finding an unexpected treasure on the map of creativity. This sense of emotion and discovery makes creativity even more rewarding and addictive.*

On our journey through Serendipities and Epiphanies, we have explored the magic of the unexpected and the beauty of the sudden revelation. These moments remind us that life is full of surprises and that, often, our greatest revelations come when we least expect them.
Serendipities guide us towards invaluable connections, while Epiphanies illuminate our path with understanding and clarity.

Let's embrace these experiences as gifts from the universe —remembering that there is always room for the unexpected in the midst of everyday life.

34

The Superpower of the Subconscious Mind

"Knowledge and access to the Subconscious Mind could be a powerful tool for self-discovery and personal change"

"You are the Alchemist of your reality, turning thoughts into things and dreams into destiny"

The Subconscious Mind

The subconscious mind is an essential part of our being that tirelessly works beneath the level of conscious awareness. It serves as a storehouse of information, beliefs, memories, emotions, and behavior patterns that significantly influence our lives. This aspect of the mind is constantly at work, even when we are not aware of it, playing a crucial role in decision-making, habit formation, and the manifestation of our reality. The subconscious acts as a filter processing the information and experiences we accumulate throughout life, creating deep-seated beliefs and thought patterns that can be both constructive and limiting. Often, these underlying beliefs can influence our actions and reactions powerfully, often without our awareness.

Understanding and accessing the subconscious mind can be a powerful tool for self-discovery and personal change. By comprehending how it operates and how its patterns can be reprogrammed, we can unlock its potential to enhance our lives and achieve our goals.

Reprogramming the Subconscious Mind

This is a process through which we can modify or change the deeply rooted thought patterns, beliefs, and behaviors in our subconscious mind. These patterns can be limiting or negative, often resulting from past experiences or external influences. Reprogramming involves the deliberate and repetitive introduction of new thoughts, beliefs, and positive affirmations into the subconscious mind to replace negative patterns. This process is fundamentally an act of self-transformation and self-empowerment. Common techniques for subconscious mind reprogramming include visualization, repeating positive affirmations, meditation, and hypnosis. These practices help create new neural pathways in the brain, allowing positive thoughts and beliefs to take root and become part of our underlying belief system.

Reprogramming the subconscious mind is essential to unleash human potential and overcome self-imposed limitations. It's a continuous process that requires patience and perseverance, but the results can be transformative, enabling us to create a reality more aligned with our desires and goals.

Reconfiguring the Subconscious Mind and Breaking Negative Habits

The subconscious mind is like an internal operating system that governs much of our daily actions and reactions. It's programmed with a set of thought patterns and beliefs we've accumulated throughout our lives. Some of these patterns are helpful, aiding us in functioning efficiently in the world, while others may be limiting and self-sabotaging. When we talk about reconfiguring the subconscious mind, we refer to the ability to change these deeply ingrained thought patterns and beliefs, especially those that are negative or self-destructive. This involves deactivating old mental circuits and building new ones.

__Neuropeptides:__ To better understand how this reconfiguration works, it's essential to talk about neuropep-

tides. Neuropeptides or peptides are small proteins that act as chemical messengers in the brain. They are released in response to our thoughts and emotions. When we think negatively or have limiting beliefs, our brain releases neuropeptides related to stress and anxiety. These neuropeptides reinforce negative thought patterns, creating a destructive cycle. However, when we reconfigure our subconscious mind, we can change this process. By adopting more positive thoughts and beliefs, we begin to release neuropeptides associated with calmness and happiness. This not only makes us feel better but also strengthens the new positive thought patterns, helping us successfully break negative habits.

In summary, reconfiguring the subconscious mind is a process of releasing negative thought patterns and beliefs and replacing them with more positive ones. Understanding how neuropeptides are involved in this process allows us to use this knowledge to create lasting change in our lives. Among the well-known peptides are endorphins, which are involved in pain regulation and the feeling of well-being, and oxytocin, often called the "love hormone" as it strengthens bonds and increases attraction and attachment in romantic partners. Its importance in regulating social behaviors and emotional responses should also be highlighted.

Positive Internal Dialogue: *Positive internal dialogue, also known as "self-talk," is the conversation we have with ourselves in our minds. This inner voice can* *be our greatest ally or our harshest critic. What we say to ourselves has a profound impact on our self-image and how we perceive the world around us.*

When we practice positive internal dialogue, we speak to ourselves in a kind and encouraging manner. Instead of focusing on our mistakes or weaknesses, we concentrate on our strengths and achievements. This doesn't mean ignoring areas where we can improve but addressing them from a place of self-compassion and growth. Positive internal dialogue is essential for the reconfiguration of the subconscious mind. When we speak to ourselves with love and support, we reinforce positive thought patterns and release neuropeptides associated with positive emotions. This, in turn, strengthens our ability to break negative habits and adopt new beliefs and behaviors.

Autosuggestion as a Tool for Change

Autosuggestion is a technique that involves repeating positive affirmations or messages to ourselves with the purpose of influencing our subconscious mind. This practice is based on the principle that our words and thoughts have a profound impact on our reality. When we autosuggest positively, we are planting seeds in the garden of our subconscious mind, creating a solid foundation for reconfiguration and change.

To use autosuggestion effectively, it's important to follow some key steps:

Define clear goals: *Before starting with autosuggestion, it's crucial to have clarity about what we want to change or achieve. This will allow us to create specific, goal-focused affirmations.*

Create positive affirmations: *Affirmations are positive, present-tense statements reflecting our goals. For example, if we want to improve our self-confidence, an affirmation could be: "I am a confident and capable person." It's important that affirmations are positive, affirmative, and meaningful to us. The "I am" statement, when accompanied by what you want to be or feel, becomes a powerful tool for co-creation, rich in profound meaning.*

Constant repetitions: *Autosuggestion requires consistency. Dedicate time every day to repeat your affirmations. You can do it aloud or silently, but make sure you are fully present in the process and feel the truth of the words you say, backed by consistent actions.*

Emotion and visualization: *To enhance autosuggestion, it's beneficial to add emotion and visualization. Feel the emotion behind your affirmations and visualize how your life would be if they were true. This will strengthen the impact on your subconscious mind.*

Positive Thought Patterns

Autosuggestion is a way of replacing negative thought patterns with positive ones. As you continue practicing, you'll notice that your internal dialogue becomes more positive and encouraging. You'll be able to observe changes in your perception and your day-to-day life.

> **Persistence:** Changes in the subconscious mind can take time. It's important to be persistent and patient in your autosuggestion practice. Over time, you'll notice how your beliefs and behaviors begin to align with your affirmations.

Autosuggestion is a powerful tool for the reconfiguration of the subconscious mind. As we incorporate positive affirmations into our daily lives, we are shaping our reality and opening the door to the manifestation of our deepest desires.

Thought Patterns and Their Impact on Reality

Our thought patterns are like paths etched in the landscape of our subconscious mind. Throughout our lives, we've developed thought patterns based on our experiences, beliefs, and perceptions.
These patterns can be positive and negative—and they have a direct impact on how we experience reality. Negative thought patterns can act as obstacles on our path to conscious creation. These patterns often include self-criti-

cal thoughts, self-doubt, fear of failure, or a belief in scarcity. When we allow these patterns to dominate our subconscious mind, we create a reality where we face constant challenges and limitations.

On the other hand, positive thought patterns can be powerful allies in conscious creation. These patterns include self-confidence, gratitude, a belief in abundance, and an affirmation that we deserve the best. When we cultivate these patterns in our subconscious mind, we open the door to attracting experiences and opportunities that reflect these positive beliefs.

The Importance of Awareness: The key to changing our thought patterns lies in awareness. We must be conscious of the thoughts passing through our minds and how they make us feel. Awareness gives us the ability to identify negative patterns and deliberately replace them with more positive and constructive thoughts.

Here are some steps to cultivate greater awareness of your thought patterns:

***Meditation and Mindfulness:** Meditation and mindfulness are effective practices to tune into your thoughts. Dedicate time each day to meditate or reflect, observing your thoughts without judgment.*

***Keeping a Journal:** Maintaining a thought journal can help identify recurring patterns. Write down your thou-*

ghts and emotions throughout the day. Try free writing, letting your thoughts flow, and you might discover some creative surprises.

Questioning Your Beliefs: *If you identify a negative thought, ask yourself if it's genuinely true. Challenge your beliefs and look for evidence supporting or refuting them.*

Practicing Gratitude: *Daily, take a moment to list things you're grateful for. This shifts focus from scarcity to abundance.*

Positive Affirmations: *As mentioned earlier, affirmations are effective tools to replace negative thought patterns. Identify negative patterns and create affirmations to counteract them.*

Changing thought patterns takes time and practice, but it's a valuable investment in your ability to consciously create the reality you desire. As you become more aware of your thoughts and choose to cultivate positive patterns, you'll experience a profound transformation in your life and your ability to manifest your deepest desires.

Recognizing Patterns in the Subconscious Mind

One of the most fascinating aspects of the subconscious mind is its ability to recognize patterns. Our minds are wired to identify connections and similarities between different experiences and events. When it comes to consciously co-creating our reality, pattern recognition plays a fundamental role. Here are some key aspects to consider:

Identifying Negative Patterns: The first step in changing negative thought patterns is recognizing them. Pay attention to recurring thoughts hindering your progress, such as patterns of self-criticism, fear, or doubt.

Examining Origins: Once you identify a negative pattern, explore where it comes from. Did it originate from a past experience? Was it inherited from someone else? Understanding a pattern's origin can help address it more effectively.

Countering with Positive Patterns: The next step is to replace negative patterns with positive ones. This is where subconscious mind reprogramming comes into play. Use affirmations, visualization, and self-suggestion to cultivate positive thought patterns.

Maintaining Awareness: As you work on changing thought patterns, it's crucial to maintain constant awareness. Negative patterns may resurface, but if you're conscious of them, you can counteract them immediately.

Observing Synchronicities: As you delve into conscious creation, you may begin noticing synchronicities *and meaningful connections in your life. These are signs that you're in tune with positive thought patterns and aligned with your desires.*

Persistence: *Changing thought patterns takes time and persistence. The subconscious mind tends to cling to the familiar, even if it's negative. With determination and consistent practice, you can reconfigure your subconscious mind to work in your favor.*
By recognizing and working with patterns in your subconscious mind, you become the architect of your reality. You have the power to transform limiting thoughts into empowering beliefs. As you immerse yourself in this process, you'll experience a profound transformation in your life and your ability to consciously create the reality you desire.

Consciousness, Miracles, and Matter
The Great Superpower of the Subconscious Mind

In this section, we'll explore how the subconscious mind plays a crucial role in creating the reality we experience. Our subconscious mind is often described as an engine behind the scenes, propelling the events and circumstances that manifest in our conscious life.

The Subconscious Mind as Reality Creator

Our subconscious mind is in constant communication with the universe, emitting signals and vibrations that attract experiences and opportunities. Here are some key points to understand how this process works:

Energetic Emissions: *Every thought we have, especially those infused with emotion, emits an energetic vibration. These vibrations act like magnets, drawing situations and people resonating with the energy we emit.*

Beliefs and Programming: *Much of the programming of the subconscious mind comes from ingrained beliefs acquired throughout our lives. These beliefs can be limiting or empowering. If we deeply believe in our ability to achieve something, our subconscious mind tirelessly works to make it a reality.*

Mind-Body Connection: *Our subconscious mind also influences our health and well-being. It can affect how we perceive pain, our recovery ability, and our immune system. It's a reminder that our physical reality is intricately connected to our mind.*

Miracles and Conscious Manifestation: *The subconscious mind can also be seen as the source of what is often called "miracles" or conscious manifestation. Here, "miracle" refers to unexpected events or outcomes that seem beyond logical explanation. However, from a conscious creation perspective, these "miracles" are the result of a subconscious mind aligned with deep belief and clear intention.*

Manifestation Practice

To consciously utilize the power of the subconscious mind in manifestation, it is essential to:

Clarity of Intent: Clearly define what you want to create or experience.

Empowering Beliefs: Identify and change limiting beliefs that may hinder your manifestation.

Visualization and Emotion: Use visualization and emotion to program your subconscious mind with the reality you desire to see materialized.

Inspired Action: Take practical steps toward your goal when you feel clear inspiration or intuition.

The subconscious mind is the link between our consciousness and the manifestation of our reality. When we understand and work with this powerful aspect of our mind, we become active co-creators of our life. "Miracles" are no longer random events but predictable outcomes of our understanding and application of this process.

Diving Deeper into the Subconscious Mind

The Inner Self and Divine Consciousness

This section'll delve even deeper into the power of the subconscious mind, exploring concepts such as the Inner Self, Divine Consciousness, and Consciousness Coherence.

The Inner Self

This is the aspect of ourselves that resides deep within the subconscious mind. It is the part of us connected to the source of all creation. Here are some key ideas:

> ***Humanity as the Microcosm of the Macrocosm:** Ancient philosophy often asserted that humanity is the microcosm of the macrocosm, meaning that we carry within us the entirety of the universe. This idea highlights that all forces and energies present in the cosmos are also present within us, especially in our Inner Self.*
>
> ***The Jewel of Creation:** We are considered the "jewel of creation" because we have the unique ability to be aware of our own existence and co-create our reality. This conscious awareness sets us apart from other forms of life.*
>
> ***All Planes of Creation:** It is said that we carry all planes of creation within us. This means that, at the subconscious level, we have access to levels of knowledge and*

wisdom far beyond our conscious understanding. This is an infinite source of creative potential.

Awakening and the Enlightenment Process: *Awakening refers to the process of becoming aware of our Inner Self and recognizing its connection to Divine Consciousness or the Universal. It is a process that involves expanding consciousness beyond the limits of the conscious mind.*

Divine Consciousness: *Divine Consciousness refers to the universal intelligence underlying everything. Some traditions call it God, others call it the Universe or Cosmos, but ultimately, it is the source of all creation. Through awakening, we realize that we are connected to this source of everything.*

The Power of the Mind in Modern Times: *Today, we are rediscovering the power of the mind through science and spirituality. Practices like meditation, visualization, and others help us access deeper levels of consciousness and harness the power of our subconscious mind.*

Consciousness Coherence and Mental Imagery: *Consciousness coherence refers to the harmony between our conscious and subconscious beliefs. When our beliefs and thoughts are aligned, we can materialize our intentions more easily.*
Mental imagery involves creating visual representations in our minds. These images can be powerful tools to in-

> *fluence our subconscious mind. When we combine clear mental images with positive beliefs and emotions, we are on the path to effective materialization.*

In summary, exploring the Inner Self, Divine Consciousness, and Consciousness Coherence helps us understand how to harness the power of the subconscious mind to co-create the reality we desire. As we awaken to this understanding, we are on the path to enlightenment, illumination, and realization of our potential as conscious creators.

Coherence of Consciousness and Mental Imagery

Receiving, perceiving, and transmitting thoughts
Divine communication on alternate planes

Here, we explore how the subconscious mind serves as a conduit, receiving, sensing, and dispatching thoughts for divine communication on different planes.

> **Receiving thoughts**
> The subconscious mind is inherently receptive and can capture thoughts and impressions from people, the environment, and, in some cases, divine sources.
>
> > ***Telepathic connection:*** *Telepathy, the conveyance of thoughts or emotions sans physical senses, finds its roots in the subconscious mind. Deep relaxation or meditation can heighten receptivity to thoughts from others.*

Intuition: The subconscious mind often imparts intuitive insights, an immediate understanding devoid of logical reasoning. This may come as hunches, premonitions, or that "gut feeling."

Receiving divine messages: Viewed as the channel for divine messages, the subconscious mind can deliver insights through dreams, visions, or moments of profound revelation.

Perceiving thoughts

The subconscious mind can also sense thoughts or energies in the environment, expressed through:

Empathy: The highly empathic subconscious mind tunes into the emotional energies of those nearby.

Energetic sensitivity: Some can feel subtle energies, perceiving spiritual entities or sensing the quality of energy in specific places.

Sending thoughts

Beyond reception, the subconscious mind can dispatch thoughts or intentions into the universe.

Power of intention: By establishing a clear and focused intention, our subconscious collaborates with the universe to materialize our desires.

> *Creative visualization:* Crafting vivid mental images of desired experiences aids the subconscious in manifesting them in reality.

Divine communication on alternate planes
The subconscious mind acts as a conduit for communication with spiritual guides, angels, or higher entities, manifesting through dreams, channeling, or altered states of consciousness.

The subconscious mind is like a bridge that connect us with other minds, energies and other planes of existence. Through our subconscious mind, we can receive, perceive, and send thoughts, which allows us to participate in divine communication that transcends the limits of the conscious mind.

Consciousness

In our exploration of conscious creation's physics of possibilities, the spotlight turns to consciousness—a compelling force steering our experiences and creations. But what is consciousness, and how does it mold our reality?

> *The science of possibilities:* Quantum physics unveils the realm of possibilities, asserting that everything is potential until observed. Conscious creation hinges on your Perception.

The secret lies in your perception—what you believe about yourself and the world, evoking a cascade of chemical and emotional responses. This causal process is pivotal in understanding how beliefs and thoughts shape reality.

The chemistry of emotion and thought: *Each emotion and thought has a biochemical foundation, influencing your emotional state and your perception and responses to the world. For example, when you feel happy, your body releases biochemical substances, and the same happens when you feel stressed out or anxious. These biochemical responses not only affect your emotional state but also influence the way you perceive and respond to the world.*

A dance between perception and reaction: *Consciousness and perception initiate a constant dance, where your beliefs and thoughts trigger biochemical and emotional responses, steering your experience.*
If you perceive that you are capable and worthy of success, this will activate the cascade of biochemical and emotional responses that propel you to achieve your goals. On the other hand, if you perceive that you're not capable, it will activate a chain of responses that could stop your progress.

The power of your mind in action: *Your mind, a reality laboratory, conducts experiments through thoughts* *and perceptions. Understanding this interplay empowers you to consciously co-create your reality.*

Coherence of consciousness: *Achieving a harmonious coherence between thoughts, emotions, and actions magnetizes desired outcomes, ushering you into a "flow state" where opportunities unfold effortlessly.*

Mental images: Visualization, a potent tool

In conscious creation, involves creating clear mental images of goals and desires, directing the subconscious mind.

Breaking the cycle of perpetual emotions: *Emotional memories can perpetuate cycles, but understanding the interplay between consciousness and emotions empowers you to redirect your mind positively.*
Each time you expose yourself to something that reminds you of that emotion—your body releases chemical substances—the peptides that reinforce that emotion create a "chemical memory" in your mind and body. For example, if you experience intense fear in a specific place—such as an elevator, you may feel that same fear every time you return to that place, even if there is no real threat. It is an example of how your emotional reactions can be perpetuated.

Emotional habits and their influence: *Emotional patterns can become addictions, trapping us in negative* *cycles. For example, some people will trigger situations or emotional self-harm just because they are addicted to those emotions, like pain and suffering—they perceive those feelings as familiar and normal.*

The thought and emotion cycle is intertwined with your body chemistry—when you understand how this works, you are capable of breaking the negative emotional habits and steering yourself to the positive seas of the mind.

Breaking these cycles and utilizing the science of consciousness depends on your willpower, persistence, and self-love.

The New Alchemy of your Subconscious Mind

The subconscious mind is an alchemical workshop where thoughts, emotions, and beliefs blend in a cosmic dance. Here, old constraints transmute into limitless possibilities—a space where dreams turn tangible through the alchemy of intention.

In this New Alchemy, you become the "wizard" of your life, transforming doubt into confidence and fear into the radiant light of love and creation.

Miracles

Definition, Evidence, and Philosophy Throughout History

Definition of Miracles

A miracle is an extraordinary phenomenon or event often perceived as a divine or supernatural act, inexplicable and transcending natural laws. These events may include miraculous healings, sudden transformations, or manifestations that defy logic and science. Miracles are commonly seen as divine interventions in the human world.

Evidence of Miracles

Throughout history, numerous accounts of miracles have been recorded in different cultures and religions. This evidence ranges from biblical miracles, such as Jesus multiplying loaves and fishes, to miraculous experiences shared by ordinary people in everyday life.

> *Religious miracles: Major religions often feature stories of miracles performed by their central figures. For example, in Christianity, miracles by Jesus, like walking on water or raising the dead, are highlighted.*

> *Personal experiences: Many individuals claim to have experienced miracles in their own lives, ranging from re-*

markable recoveries from illnesses to events that seemingly protect people from imminent dangers.

Philosophy of Miracles

The philosophy of miracles is a complex topic often approached from different perspectives:

> ***Religious belief:*** *For many, miracles manifest divine power and confirm their religious faith. These events serve as evidence of the existence of a supreme being and their influence on the world.*
>
> ***Scientific interpretation:*** *From a scientific standpoint, miracles are often explained as rare but natural events not yet fully understood. It is argued that science is continually evolving, and what is considered a "miracle" today may have a scientific explanation in the future.*
>
> ***Skeptical questioning:*** *Some adopt a skeptical attitude toward miracles, arguing that many of these events can be explained through psychological phenomena, coincidences, or simply a lack of solid evidence.*

DNA of Miracles and Evidences

The "DNA" of miracles—I use this term to refer to the common characteristics shared by these events, such as extreme improbability or the ability to transform lives. Miracles often leave a profound impact on those who experience them and those who hear about them.

Notable examples of miracles throughout history highlight their implications and how the perception of miracles can vary based on individual perspectives and beliefs. We can also observe how miracles often challenge our current understanding of the world and its natural laws, posing fascinating questions about the relationship between the divine and the human.

> *Miracles and the evolution of human perception:* Miracles have played a very significant role in the evolution of human perception and the shaping of our spiritual and religious beliefs. Throughout history, these events have been sources of inspiration, hope, and wonder, influencing how we view the world and our relationship with the divine.
>
> *Spiritual inspiration:* Miracles often serve as sources of inspiration for people from various spiritual traditions. They reinforce faith and belief in a higher power that intervenes in human life. Miracle stories have been instrumental in the formation of religions and belief systems.
>
> *Reflection on the unknown:* Miracles also remind us that our knowledge is limited. When confronted with events that seem to defy natural laws, we are faced with the idea that there is much we still don't understand about the universe and its functioning.

Search for meaning: *Miracles often trigger a search for meaning in individuals. Why did they happen? What is their purpose? These questions have led to profound philosophical and spiritual explorations about the meaning of life and our existence in the cosmos.*

Impact on culture: *The influence of miracles extends beyond the spiritual realm to culture and art. Miracles have been recurring themes in literature, painting, and music, contributing to the richness of human expression.*

Evolution of science: *As scientific knowledge advances, some events that were once considered miraculous have found rational explanations. This has led to an ongoing debate about the relationship between science and faith, as well as how the perception of miracles has evolved over time.*

Miracles have been a powerful force in shaping human culture and spirituality, as well as in how we understand our place in the universe.

Evidences

Evidence, in my context, refers to tangible manifestations of miracles, palpable confirmations that I have tuned into the right frequency to attract what I desire. This may include events or circumstances that, from my perspective, are challenging to explain conventionally and are perceived as results of synchronicity or divine intervention.

Miracle evidence is like fireflies in the night of uncertainty, small lights flashing in the darkness to remind us that even in the most challenging moments, the magic of the inexplicable can weave its cloak of hope, love, and healing over our lives.

Matter

Matter is everything that occupies space and has mass. In other words, it is everything you can touch and physically feel. Matter is composed of subatomic particles, such as atoms and molecules, which interact with each other through electromagnetic and nuclear forces. Matter can exist in different states as solid, liquid, and gas, depending on how particles are organized and how they interact. It can also change from one state to another through processes like fusion and vaporization.

In the context of discussing the power of the mind and matter, there is often reference to how our thoughts and beliefs can influence the materialization of physical events or circumstances in our lives. This suggests that the mind plays a role in interacting with matter at levels deeper than what we normally perceive in our daily experience.

Mind and Matter: Creating Abundance and Awakening Superpowers

On the journey to explore the powers of the subconscious mind, we cannot overlook the extraordinary relationship between the mind and matter. This relationship is like a bridge between the inner world of our thoughts and the outer world we experience daily. The idea that our thoughts can influence matter may seem like a premise from a science fiction movie, but it is a concept deeply rooted in understanding reality and abundance. As we delve into this chapter, we will open the door to the notion that our minds have the power to create, shape, and manifest matter itself. Let's explore this intriguing connection between consciousness and matter, and discover how this understanding can open doors to abundance and the superpowers that lie within each of us.

Matter and Consciousness: In the mystical theater of existence, matter and consciousness engage in a hypnotic dance. Imagine this: the stage is set with the grand tapestry of the universe, woven with threads of cosmic energy. On one side, you have matter, the silent actor taking cues from the director of consciousness. On the other, consciousness, the master of this cosmic ballet, choreographs the movements of matter with the precision of a masterful director.

Matter, the tangible manifestation of energy, follows the guidelines of consciousness. It responds to the thoughts, beliefs, and intentions that consciousness projects onto the stage. This interaction is the very essence of creation. In this dance, the stage becomes a canvas, and matter becomes the paint. Every thought, every emotion, every intention is a stroke on this canvas, creating the masterpiece of our reality. Imagine, for a moment, that your mind is a brush, and your thoughts are the colors you choose. What image are you painting on the grand theater of life? Is it a masterpiece of joy, abundance, and love, or a darker representation of fear and limitation?

This dance between matter and consciousness is not limited by the constraints of time and space. It unfolds in the eternal now, where the past, present, and future coexist in a harmonious symphony. What you believe and imagine in this moment sends waves through the fabric of reality, shaping the past and influencing the future.

Abundance and Superpowers: Unveiling Your Creative Potential

Now, let's talk about abundance and superpowers. You see, in this dance of matter and consciousness, you possess the incredible ability to co-create your reality. Your mind is not just a brush but a "magic wand" that can materialize your deepest desires. Abundance flows from the recognition that the cosmos is an infinite canvas, and you are the artist. You can paint a life full of prosperity, love, and satisfaction. All you need is the belief that you deserve it, the intention to create it, and the inspired action to bring it to life.

As for superpowers, think of them as the extraordinary abilities you have within you, waiting to be unleashed. These are not just the stuff of comics but the hidden potential of your consciousness. From the intuition guiding your decisions to the healing power that mends your wounds, you possess a variety of superpowers beyond your imagination. The key is to awaken your innate abilities, trust in the dance of matter and consciousness, and embrace your role as both creator and creation. As you do, you'll discover that...

"you are the alchemist of your reality, turning thoughts into things and dreams into destiny."

I refer to the internal superpowers we all carry within, in the depths of our minds and consciousness. These are not magical powers in the conventional sense but the amazing capabilities of our subconscious mind to shape the reality we experience. Have you ever wondered why some people seem to have a streak of good luck while others always face challenges? The key lies in understanding how our subconscious mind works in harmony with the universe to manifest our thoughts and beliefs.

Within each of us lies a treasure trove of untapped potential, a source of power that transcends understanding—these are the superpowers of the human spirit, the ability to transform, create, heal. As alchemists of our reality, we have the gift of turning thoughts into things and dreams into destiny. So, embrace these internal powers, awaken their magic, and watch as your life evolves, transforming into a journey of wonders and infinite possibilities.

35

Beyond Reality

Quantum Physics and Parallel Universes

"These moments when we take conscious control of our reality, navigating the infinite possibilities before us, remind us of our 'power' to shape our existence and materialize the destiny we so yearn for"

Quantum physics is the field of physics that study systems at microscopic scales, where quantum effects are significant. It examines the behavior of subatomic particles such as electrons and photons, characterized by phenomena like wave-particle duality and superposition, significantly differing from classical physics.

Parallel Universes: Known as the "multiverse" theory, it is an interpretation of quantum mechanics suggesting that for every possible quantum outcome, the universe branches, creating a parallel universe where each outcome occurs. In other words, every choice you make could lead to multiple realities, each with its version of events.

Quantum Leaps: A quantum leap refers to a discrete transition between subatomic energy levels without passing through intermediate states from one level to another; the electron jumps directly from one to another.

Reflections on Parallel Universes and Quantum Leaps:

At the heart of quantum mechanics, we encounter a theory that challenges our intuition and redefines our understanding of the world. To delve into quantum mechanics and parallel universes, we must start by considering those pioneers who ventured into this unknown territory.

> **Pioneers of Quantum Mechanics:** In the first half of the 20th century, scientists like Max Planck, Niels Bohr, and Werner Heisenberg laid the foundations of quantum mechanics. What they discovered was extraordinary: at subatomic scales, the world is remarkably different from what we perceive daily. This subatomic particle can exist in multiple places simultaneously, and its behavior is inherently probabilistic.

The Enigma of Superposition: One of the most surprising concepts is superposition. Imagine tossing a coin in the air; instead of landing heads or tails, in the quantum world, the coin would be in a state of superposition, being both things simultaneously until observed. This principle leads us to an intriguing question: do multiple realities exist where all possibilities come true?

Parallel Universes and the Multiverse: The idea of parallel universes is based on this notion. According to this interpretation, every choice we make and every possible quantum outcome give rise to the creation of parallel universes. You might take the left path in one, while in another, you take the right. In this vast multiverse, all possibilities unfold.

Quantum Leaps and Linear Time: In this fascinating world, quantum leaps are like small transitions between realities. But here's the real wonder: from the quantum perspective, linear time as we know it becomes an illusion. All these parallel universes coexist simultaneously with their different choices and outcomes. Each moment and choice is a point in the vast tapestry of time and space.

Quantum Time Travel: One of the most intriguing concepts is the possibility of quantum time travel. Although this may sound like a science fiction plot, quantum mechanics raises some intriguing questions about the nature of time. If time is an illusion, could we someday master quantum leaps to explore the past or the future? While this is still speculative, we can't help but dream of the possibilities this could open.

Mandela Effect and Subjective Reality: Another interesting perspective is the Mandela Effect, where people remember historical events differently from how they are recorded in reality. Could this be evidence of reality changes due to quantum leaps? This leads to an even deeper question: is reality objective or subjective? Can we influence our reality simply by changing our perspective?

Quantum Leaps in Everyday Life: Although quantum leaps belong to the realm of the subatomic, they might be closer to us than we think. In our lives, we often experience decisive moments that radically change our course. Are these moments simply the result of our individual choices, or could they be manifestations of quantum leaps in action?

In the vastness of human experience, it is speculated that our destinies are intertwined with a series of conscious or unconscious 'quantum leaps' that take us from one state of being to another. These are constantly happening in unimaginable ways.

In these moments, when we take conscious control

of our reality, navigating the infinite possibilities before us, they remind us of our 'power' to shape our own existence and materialize that destiny we long for.

Quantum Connection with Spirituality: Finally, we will explore how these ideas intertwine with spirituality and the search for meaning. Some argue that quantum leaps could be a way to explain profound spiritual experiences or seemingly inexplicable phenomena.

As we delve into the world of parallel universes and quantum leaps, I invite you to keep an open mind and a perspective of wonder. What we discover here could fundamentally change how we view the world and our own existence. This is a journey into the unknown, and together, we will explore the frontiers of reality and consciousness. Get ready for an exciting and transformative journey!

The Influence of Consciousness: In recent years, an intriguing debate has emerged about whether human consciousness can influence quantum events. Some argue that conscious observation can collapse the quantum wave function and determine the outcome of an experiment. This raises significant philosophical questions about the relationship between the mind and reality. Could our consciousness have a direct impact on the fabric of the universe?

The Mystery of "Non-Locality": Non-locality is another surprising phenomenon in quantum mechanics. This means that quantum particles can be instantly connected to each other regardless of the distance that separates them. In other words, one particle can "know" what another is doing, even if they are light-years apart. This mystery challenges our traditional understanding of causality and suggests a profound interconnection in the fabric of the universe.

Our level of human understanding may help clarify why we can perceive other people related to us in an unexplainable way, regardless of distance or time.

Reflections on Reality: Quantum mechanics challenges us to question the very nature of reality. What is real, and what is illusory? In the quantum world, particles can exist in multiple states simultaneously, and measurements can influence what we observe. This leads us to contemplate whether reality is objective or co-created by our observation and consciousness.

Mind-Matter Connection: The idea that consciousness can influence quantum events raises profound questions about the relationship between the mind and matter. How can our seemingly immaterial mind affect the behavior of subatomic particles? This enigma leads us to explore the nature of consciousness and its role in co-creating reality.

Reality Beyond Reality: By exploring quantum physics and multiverses, we venture into territories where our conventional notions of cause and effect may crumble. This challenges us to consider that reality may be much more expansive and mysterious than we generally perceive—something beyond our current understanding.

The Fabric of Space-Time: To understand quantum leaps and parallel universes, we must delve into the very fabric of space-time. Imagine time not as an arrow moving in a single direction but as a vast, boundless ocean where each moment coexists. In this ocean, our choices and actions can be seen as diverging paths, creating branches in the temporal flow.

To illustrate these ideas, consider the Schrödinger's cat experiment. In this thought experiment, a cat is in a box with a radioactive particle. According to quantum mechanics, until we open the box and observe the cat, it is in a superposition state, meaning it is simultaneously alive and dead. This paradox challenges our intuition but illustrates how observation affects reality at the quantum level.

The Quantum Observer: Another intriguing idea is that of the "quantum observer." Quantum mechanics suggests that the observer's consciousness plays a fundamental role in determining a quantum outcome. It raises a profound question about the nature of consciousness and how our mind can influence the reality we experience simply by observing or creating mental images of the reality we wish to experience.

The Multiverse and Timelines: Parallel universes result from the multiverse theory. According to this idea, every choice we make and every event that occurs can lead to the creation of a new universe. In one universe, you might take one path while you make a different decision in another. This implies that our lives are intertwined with multiple timelines, each representing a different version of our story. It is also said that we can make quantum leaps from one parallel world to another, explaining why sometimes we feel lost or don't recognize changes in our reality—the explanation is that unknowingly, we are moving from one timeline to another. It is a fascinating hypothesis that personally motivates me to investigate and experiment more deeply.

Today, science fiction is closer to showing us, through more knowledge and high technology, these fascinating theories or future laws of microcosmic physics.

The Importance of Consciousness: As we explore these concepts, we realize that consciousness is more than a passive spectator of reality. Our consciousness can be an active force in creating our life experiences. This leads us to consider our responsibility in choosing our perceptions and beliefs, as these can shape the reality we experience.

In this journey through microcosmic physics and parallel universes, I invite you to keep an open and curious mind. These ideas challenge conventional notions of how the world works and offer a fascinating framework for understanding our existence.
I encourage you to reflect on their meaning in your own life and consider how to apply these perspectives to your quest for self-discovery, transformation, and evolution.

36

Quantum Psychology

Navigating the Subatomic Seas of the Mind

"Quantum Psychology is the understanding that time and space are not linear within the Quantum or Subatomic Realm"

In the previous chapters, we set sail across the boundless ocean of consciousness realms, unveiling the intricate dance where our thoughts and beliefs sculpt the canvas of the world. We journeyed into the profound connection between our inner self and the outer tapestry of reality, discovering the enchanting power of perception and intention.

As we navigate into the depths of Quantum Psychology, get ready to voyage even further into the enigmas of the mind and the cosmos. This chapter acts as a bridge between the familiar and the unknown, a sojourn into the subatomic seas of consciousness, where the laws of quantum mechanics hold sway.

Defining Quantum Psychology

At its core, Quantum Psychology is the science and theory that probes the nature, implications, and relationships woven within the tapestry of our consciousness. It's a psychological approach seeking to integrate and explore the facets of our mind governed by the laws of quantum mechanics, all while dancing with the rhythms of our broader consciousness, following the well-known Newtonian physical laws and social experiences.

> **Beyond the Newtonian paradigm:** One of Quantum Psychology's main revelations is the realization that time and space aren't linear in the Quantum or Subatomic Kingdom. From this perspective, our Quantum Self gains the ability to perceive and decide based on events in this extraordinary plane of existence. It's a realm where our thoughts and intentions mingle with subatomic particles flowing through us and the entire universe. Furthermore, once this connection is established, time and space constraints no longer wield the same power as in our Newtonian everyday reality.
>
> **The impact on daily life:** So why should we care about the nuanced aspects of the Quantum Realm in our daily

lives? The answer lies in the profound implications this understanding holds for us. It reshapes how we see our place in the world, make decisions, and co-create our reality. It's akin to a magical key unlocking the door to a new way of being, where we become co-creators with the universe itself.

Implications for daily life

Now that we've laid the groundwork for Quantum Psychology, let's explore how this understanding can metamorphosize our everyday lives. Here are some of the most thrilling implications:

> ***Our reality is malleable:*** *We begin to see that reality is far more malleable than we ever imagined. Our thoughts and emotions can sway the events and circumstances we encounter. As co-creators of our reality, we seize the reins of our lives.*
>
> ***Awareness of choice:*** *Quantum Psychology empowers us to make conscious choices. Instead of feeling trapped by external circumstances, we recognize that we always have options and can choose the ones that align best with our desires and values.*
>
> ***Healing and transformation:*** *We can harness this understanding for personal healing and transformation as we grasp how consciousness operates at the quantum le-*

vel. Ancient wounds and negative thought patterns can be released and replaced by healthier, more empowering patterns.

Universal connection: *We realize our deep connection to the universe and others. We are an integral part of the web of life, and our actions and thoughts reverberate across the whole. This fosters a sense of responsibility and compassion towards ourselves and others.*

Unlimited potential: *Quantum Psychology reminds us of our boundless potential. Our current circumstances or past don't confine us. We can manifest a reality more aligned with our desires by focusing on what we want to create and believing it's possible.*

Quantum mechanics and consciousness: *A pivotal concept in Quantum Psychology is the dance between quantum mechanics and consciousness. Quantum mechanics, the theory governing subatomic particles, suggests that consciousness itself can influence the quantum world. In the quantum realm, particles can exist in multiple states simultaneously and shift state in response to observation. This is raising profound questions about the role of the mind and consciousness in shaping reality. To what extent do our observations and thoughts ripple through the quantum world? Can consciousness influence reality on a broader scale? We'll explore these questions and witness how Quantum Psychology unfolds a new* *understanding of the mind and its relationship with the universe. As we dive into these concepts, we invite you to keep an open and receptive mind because what you uncover may fundamentally alter how you experience and perceive life.*

The roots of Quantum Psychology: *To fully grasp Quantum Psychology, we must delve into its origins and evolution. This field didn't sprout overnight; instead, it was nurtured by many ideas, theories, and scientific advances throughout history.*

Fundamentals of quantum mechanics: *As mentioned earlier, Quantum Psychology heavily leans on quantum mechanics, the theory unraveling the behavior of subatomic particles. Pioneers like Max Planck and Niels Bohr laid the foundations for understanding how particles can exist in multiple states and how observation influences their behavior.*

Philosophy and spirituality: *Quantum Psychology draws inspiration from Eastern philosophy and spiritual traditions. Concepts like the unity of consciousness and the interconnection of all things echo ideas in philosophies such as Buddhism and Taoism.*

New paradigms in psychology: *As psychology progressed in the 20th century, fresh perspectives emerged aligning with the principles of Quantum Psychology.*

Humanistic Psychology, for instance, concentrates on personal growth and self-realization — themes foundational to Quantum Psychology.

Studies of consciousness: *Research in fields like Parapsychology and the exploration of altered states of consciousness also contributed to the evolution of Quantum Psychology. These studies challenged conventional views of the mind and reality.*

A new paradigm of mind and reality: *One of Quantum Psychology's most thrilling aspects is that it heralds a new paradigm in understanding the mind and reality. Until recently, science and psychology operated on a reductionist model, breaking everything into smaller parts for isolated study. However, Quantum Psychology urges us to perceive the mind and reality in an entirely new light.*
Instead of breaking the mind down into its bare components, Quantum Psychology acknowledges the mind as an interconnected whole, with our experiences arising from the interplay between consciousness and the quantum world. This new paradigm challenges us to transcend the limitations of old-fashioned thinking and embrace a more holistic, unified approach.

The Implications for day-to-day life:

A common question when exploring a new approach like Quantum Psychology is, "How does this affect my daily

life?" It's a valid question since theory and philosophy must translate into practical applications to impact our lives significantly.
Quantum Psychology offers a series of practical tools to help you live a more prosperous, more authentic life.

As with any new paradigm, Quantum Psychology demands a shift in how we think and experience the world —you'll discover the potential to transform your life in unimaginable ways.

37

Quantum Healing and Energy Psychology

Discovering the Inner Power

"Cultivating humility, empathy, and understanding brings us closer to inner peace and strengthens relationships"

Embarking on this cosmic odyssey into the realms of quantum healing and energy psychology, we venture beyond the conventional boundaries of medicine and psychology. Here, the essence of our being extends far beyond the confines of our physical form—it permeates our minds and intertwines with the intricate web of subtle energies flowing through us, unveiling a remarkable and mysterious capacity for healing.

Join me on this chapter as we delve into the exploration of quantum healing and energy psychology. Together, we'll uncover the secrets of how the synergy between our mind, emotions, and energy can weave profound and unexpected threads of influence over our health and well-being.

Our journey will unfold through various quantum healing techniques, from the enchanting realms of energy medicine to the cellular tapestry of healing. Witness how the mind becomes the catalyst for self-healing, and energy becomes the sculptor, restoring balance to every facet of our existence. Discover how emotions and traumas can find refuge in our energy system, and the liberation of these energies can pave the way for profound and enduring healing.

This is not merely a journey; it's a radiant metamorphosis within. Here, you'll come to recognize your innate power as a healing artisan. Let's unfurl the mystique of quantum healing and Energy Psychology, unlocking your mind and heart to the boundless possibilities that await.

Quantum Healing: The Science of Healing Energy

To fully grasp the essence of quantum healing and Energy Psychology, let's immerse ourselves in the scientific currents that buoy them. At the core of these practices lies the profound belief that we are beings pulsating with energy, and our thoughts and emotions emit vibrations capable of shaping our health.

Zooming into the microcosmic dance of physics, we discover that everything, from distant galaxies to the tiniest cells within us, is composed of subatomic particles vibrating with energy. These particles, far from static entities, resemble probability waves capable of existing in multiple states simultaneously.

It is within this subatomic dance that the potential for quantum healing resides. Our minds, through intention, can sway these particles and, consequently, our physical, emotional, and mental well-being.

Energy medicine, encompassing practices like acupuncture and polarity therapy, rests on the premise that our body is a continuous flow of energy. Optimal health prevails when this energy flows freely, but stress, buried emotions, or traumas can obstruct this flow, giving rise to physical and emotional maladies. Enter Energy Psychology, a discipline addressing the intricate interplay between our emotions, thoughts, and our body's energy, offering keys to unlock blocks and foster healing. As we plunge deeper, we'll unravel specific quantum healing techniques, from the vivid landscapes of visualization to the serene realms of meditation and mindfulness. Learn how to wield your mind as a potent tool in sculpting your well-being.

Yet, quantum healing and Energy Psychology aren't confined to the realms of sterile science—they embrace spirituality and the intimate dance between mind and body.

Explore how your beliefs and mental states can shape your energy, aligning your intention with your higher self for profound healing.

Let's begin our journey to the understanding of our limitless healing potential.

This is the commencement of our expedition into the boundless realm where science, mind, and energy intertwine in a healing embrace. It's time to unfurl the sails and navigate the currents of quantum healing and Energy Psychology!

The Placebo Effect: The Power of Believing in Healing

As we voyage through the seas of quantum healing and Energy Psychology, a fascinating phenomenon beckons our attention—the enigmatic "placebo effect." This serves as a testament to the immense power the mind holds over the body, showcasing its ability to shape the narrative of healing.
Imagine this: You're momentarily unwell, and your doctor hands you a pill, touting it as a revolutionary and highly effective drug. Little do you know; you're actually consuming a sugar pill—a placebo. Astonishingly, with time, your symptoms start to abate and eventually vanish. How can this be?
The placebo effect is a captivating response of the body to the belief in a cure. When we place trust in a treatment, our brain orchestrates the release of chemicals and endor-

phins that influence our immune system and overall health. This phenomenon underscores the intricate connection between mind and body, showcasing how our beliefs and expectations can profoundly shape our health.

Peptides of the Immune System: Energy Communication

Within the tapestry of our body, a marvelously subtle communication system awaits acknowledgment—the peptides of the immune system. These diminutive yet potent molecules play a pivotal role in orchestrating communication between our cells and regulating our immune responses.

Peptides, akin to energetic messengers, transmit vital information across our bodies. They partake in processes ranging from inflammation to stress regulation and immune responses. What's truly fascinating is that our thoughts, emotions, and mental states hold sway over these peptides.

The peptides of the immune system are intricately linked to our consciousness, showcasing how our emotions and beliefs can directly influence these biological messengers. This realization unfolds a new panorama of possibilities—how we can wield our mental and energetic states to influence our health.

Epigenetics: The Power to Change Our Genes

Epigenetics, a captivating field, shatters the notion that our genes dictate our destiny. It illuminates the path to understanding that we possess the power to shape how our genes express themselves throughout our lives.

Envision your genes as keys on a piano, each with the potential to be played or remain silent. Some keys can toggle on or off over time, and our lifestyle choices, emotional experiences, and quantum healing practices can influence this process.

Epigenetics empowers us to reshape the narrative of our genetic expression. Discover how our choices, emotions, and quantum healing practices can influence our genetics and, consequently, our health.

By immersing ourselves in the study of the placebo effect, the peptides of the immune system, and epigenetics, we unravel the potent influence of the mind and energy in the healing process. Our journey is a profound odyssey of self-discovery and transformation, delving into the depths of our being and soaring to new heights of well-being.

The Epigenetics Revolution: Forging Our Health Destiny

As we traverse the landscapes of epigenetics, a revolution awaits—one that challenges the age-old belief that our genes decree our fate. Epigenetics unfolds a narrative where we hold the power to reshape our genetic history, forging a destiny of health and vitality in unforeseen ways.

Dive deeper into the symphony of our genes, where the melody of life is not a predetermined score but a dynamic composition influenced by our choices and experiences. In the realm of epigenetics, our genes are instruments waiting for the direction of a master conductor—us. Chemical "labels" known as epigenetic marks dance upon our genes, activated or deactivated by the intricate interplay of our lifestyle choices and experiences.

Practical Tools to Shape Genetic Expression

Let's equip ourselves with practical tools to orchestrate our genetic symphony for optimal health and well-being:

> *Mindfulness and Meditation:* Engage in regular mindfulness and meditation practices to manage stress and reduce inflammation, positively impacting the expression of health-related genes. Picture your mind as the conductor's baton, guiding the harmonious flow of genetic expression.

> *Conscious Eating:* Your diet is a brushstroke on the canvas of your genes. Choose nutrient-rich foods to promote better health and lower the risk of diseases. Become the culinary artist sculpting your genetic masterpiece.

> *Physical Exercise:* Transform your body into a kinetic masterpiece through regular exercise. Influence the expression of genes related to cardiovascular function, mental health, and more. Imagine each workout session

as a note resonating through the corridors of your genetic composition.

Emotional Management: Conduct the emotional symphony within. Healthy emotional management reduces chronic stress, positively influencing your genes. Your emotional state is the melody that shapes the genetic harmony of well-being.

Rest and Sleep: Each night's slumber is a gentle lullaby for your genes. Good quality sleep is essential for cell regeneration, impacting genetic expression related to energy and longevity. Your dreams become the whispers guiding your genetic dance.

Social Support Network: Envision your social connections as the chorus in your genetic opera. Maintaining healthy relationships to influence your mental and emotional health is a sweet serenade that resonates through the genes.

Alternative Therapies: Explore therapeutic melodies like acupuncture, herbal medicine, and homeopathy, harmonizing with improvements in health and influencing the expression of immune response genes. Let these alternative therapies be the instrumental solos in your genetic ensemble.

Spiritual and Gratitude Practices: Elevate your mental and emotional health through spiritual and gratitude *practices. These are the ethereal notes that subtly shift the genetic composition, opening doors to well-being.*

These tools are the brushes, the notes, and the guiding hands that craft the masterpiece of your genetic expression. Remember, each person is a unique artist, painting their genetic canvas with the hues of daily choices and mentality.

Emotional Expressiveness

Emotions are the vibrant palette with which we paint the canvas of our lives. Yet, the struggle to express them effectively often casts a shadow.
Embracing our emotional expressiveness is fundamental in our quest for a more stable, balanced, and healthy life. It means honoring all emotions, even the ones we consider unpleasant and embarrassing. We can learn to embrace all of our emotions as an important part of who we are.
From the brightest hues of joy to the shadowy depths of pain. Learn the dance of emotional catharsis, a liberating process that allows you to feel and express emotions fully and healthily.

Let's unravel the importance of emotional expressiveness, a crucial player in our mental and physical health.

Releasing Emotional Tension: The Liberation Dance
Our emotions, in many occasions can become a heavy load that we carry for a long time. We experience many disorganized impulses and intense accumulation of emotion cycles, like anger, fear, embarrassment and shyness.

Embrace the totality of your emotions

Each emotion, from joy to pain, is a part of our essential human experience—honoring and understanding our emotions and how we can enhance our life's experience. As we delve into the profundity of our feelings, we discover that it could be a powerful tool in the journey to a happy, significant, and fulfilling life.

Emotional Expressiveness and how to purge your Emotions

Emotional Catharsis:
When emotions become burdensome, let emotional catharsis be the gust of wind that clears the air. Cry when sadness knocks, scream in a safe space when anger boils. Seek the gentle embrace of friends or family who listen without judgment—a healing ritual for the soul.

Promotion of Happiness Hormones:
Activate the orchestra of happiness hormones—endorphins, dopamine, serotonin, oxytocin, and melatonin.

Engage in regular exercise, gratitude practices, meditation, and meaningful social connections to compose a melody of emotional well-being. Each note resonates through the corridors of joy and balance.

Avoiding Emotional Burdens: The Liberation Anthem of "No"

Learn the assertive art of saying "no" to protect your emotional well-being. Shed the burdens of unnecessary responsibilities, embracing the freedom to set healthy limits. Preserve your energy for what truly matters, a self-care act conducted with discipline and love.

The Art of Receiving: Saying "Yes" to Life's Gifts

Saying "yes" is a celebration of life. Learn to receive help, love, and support—a vital chord in the symphony of human connection. Saying "yes" to enriching experiences opens the floodgates to new possibilities and personal growth.

Forgiveness and Liberation: Releasing the Grudges' Balloon

Forgiveness is the gentle breeze that lifts the weight of grudges and anger. Free yourself from the shackles of the past, creating space for healing. Forgiveness isn't forgetting; it's choosing liberation from the negative influence of past wounds on your present and future.

Throwing Away the Suitcase of the Past: A Lighter Journey
Carrying the weight of the past can be exhausting. Let go of unfulfilled expectations, past mistakes, and regrets — the suitcase of the past. Live lighter, focus on the present, and craft a positive future.

Living in the Present: The Eternal Now
The present is the only moment we truly possess. Immerse yourself in mindfulness, savoring the moments of joy, practicing gratitude, and being completely present. Living in the present allows you to find fullness and satisfaction in the daily symphony of life.

The Power of Forgiveness: Liberation and self-forgiveness

Forgiveness, a sacred tool for spiritual and emotional healing, grants us the extraordinary ability to unburden ourselves from the weight of grudges and resentment. Let's unravel its significance and explore how to weave it into the fabric of our lives.

Releasing Grudges: Freedom in Forgiveness
Forgiveness is not about absolving others of responsibility; it's a liberation from the internal shackles of negativity and pain. Embrace forgiveness as the gentle breeze that sweeps away the emotional burdens of holding grudges.

Self-Forgiveness: Nurturing Self-Love

In the symphony of forgiveness, don't forget the crucial note of self-forgiveness. Acknowledge mistakes, embrace moments of weakness, and let self-forgiveness be the melody that releases guilt and self-criticism, fostering greater self-esteem and acceptance.

Letting Go: The Art of Liberation

Forgiveness is a dance of letting go. It liberates us from the chains of the past, creating spaciousness for new experiences and opportunities in the present. Let forgiveness be the brushstroke that transforms the canvas of your life.

Let Bygones Be Bygones: Changing Perspectives

In the realms of forgiveness, we accept that the past cannot be changed, but we have the power to change how we relate to those events. By forgiving, we shift our perspective, allowing the past to no longer cast a shadow over our present.

Living in the Present: The Tapestry of Joy and Peace

Forgiveness is the gateway to living fully in the present. As we release grudges and pain, we open ourselves to the boundless joy, love, and peace available in the here and now. Embrace the gift of the present with open arms.

A Journey of Self-Discovery: Healing Wounds and Growing

Forgiveness takes us on a profound journey of self-discovery. It prompts us to confront our wounds, fostering growth and evolution as human beings. Through forgiveness, we metamorphose into the architects of our own healing.

The Art of Letting Go: Shedding the Suitcase of the Past

Life's journey often sees us accumulating a suitcase filled with experiences, emotions, and memories—some heavy with grudges and pain. Visualize releasing this suitcase as an act of empowerment.

The Suitcase of the Past: Unloading Emotional Baggage

Imagine carrying a suitcase laden with negative emotions from the past: grudges, resentments, sadness, guilt, and fears. This suitcase grows heavier with each step on your journey. The beautiful truth? You hold the power to let it go.

Letting Go as Empowerment: Reclaiming Control

Letting go is an act of empowerment. It's the realization that you're not a prisoner of the past; you wield control over your emotions and thoughts. With each release, you reclaim a piece of your inner strength.

Release of Emotional Burdens: Lightening the Soul
By releasing grudges and resentments, you unburden yourself from the emotional weight you've carried. Experience the lightness that follows, fostering inner peace and tranquility.

The Past No Longer Defines Your Present: Embracing New Possibilities
Often, we let the past shape our present identity. Letting go of the suitcase allows you to open to new possibilities, defining yourself not by the past, but by the vibrant, evolving being you are now.

How to Drop the Suitcase: Tools for Liberation
Letting go doesn't mean forgetting or denying; it means freeing yourself from the power those experiences hold. Utilize tools like forgiveness, acceptance, and self-love to lighten the load and embark on a journey unencumbered.

Living in the Present: A Symphony of Here and Now

When the past is released, the present unfolds. Immerse yourself in the magic and beauty of each moment. Letting go paves the way for a brighter, more joyful experience of the present.

Embracing the Gift of Now
Our minds often dwell in the past or worry about the future, robbing us of the richness of the present. Learning to live in the now is a precious gift you give yourself.

The Wandering Mind
Our minds have a tendency to wander, carrying us away from the present with thoughts of worry and anxiety. Enter mindfulness, a practice that anchors you in the present moment, bringing attention to thoughts, emotions, and body sensations without judgment.

Mindfulness: Painting the Present with Awareness
It is a practice that helps you to be fully present in the present moment—and requires you to pay attention to your thoughts, emotions, and body sensations without judging them. It is a way of being aware of your experience in the present.
Practicing mindfulness regularly bestows gifts of reduced stress, increased concentration, improved mental and emotional health, and heightened life satisfaction. It's a way of painting your experience in the present, creating peace and clarity.
You can practice mindfulness at anytime and anywhere. You could start by becoming aware of your breathing, the physical sensations in your body, or the sounds surrounding you. As you become more aware of the present, you will experience a sense of peace and clarity.

The Magic of the Present: Gratitude for Every Moment
Fully living in the present unveils the magic of every moment. With gratitude, savor the simple pleasures—like a cup of hot tea or a heart-to-heart conversation with a friend.

Breaking the Illusion of Linear Time

Quantum mechanics challenges our perception of time and space. The past, present, and future coexist. Your choices and actions in the present ripple into the future, influencing your reality.

The Power of Now: Orchestrating Change and Transformation

In the embrace of the present, you become the creator of your reality. Every thought, emotion, and choice shapes your future. Quantum co-creation unveils your true power, sparking a change of perspective.

> *Change of Perspective: Challenges as Opportunities*
>
> *Living in the present shifts your perspective. Challenges cease to be obstacles; they become stepping stones to profound personal growth. Your journey transforms into an adventure of self-discovery.*
>
> *The Transformation Begins Here: Metamorphosis*
>
> *Personal and spiritual transformation unfolds not in the past or the future but in the present. Here, you can free yourself from limiting patterns and embrace your authentic essence. Quantum co-creation beckons you to be mindful of your thoughts and emotions, sculpting the reality you desire.*

The Path to Fullness: Embracing Quantum Co-Creation

As our quantum co-creation journey culminates, a profound understanding emerges: you hold the power to shape the life you want. Through releasing the past, living in the present, and gazing confidently toward the future, you stand on the threshold of fullness.

The symphony of emotional liberation and quantum co-creation continues, inviting you to dance with the magic of the present, where each note, each breath, and each choice resonates with the melody of your creation.

Cultivating Humility: A Journey to Inner Fullness

Humility, a potent quality that intertwines us with our true essence and enhances our relationships, is a virtue attainable through self-evaluation, active listening, and openness to new perspectives. Unraveling patterns hindering authenticity, nobility, and generosity is essential in this transformative journey.

Not All That Glitters Is Gold and recognizing self-destructive patterns is important. As we embark on the journey toward humility, it's crucial to identify these patterns that hinder authenticity.

Destructive traits like arrogance, envy, presumptuousness, and competitiveness cast shadows on humility's brilliance. Acknowledging these patterns is the first step toward transformation.

Addressing Envy and Obsessive Competition

Envy and obsessive competition are shadows that obscure the brilliance of humility. Recognizing and admitting them is the first step towards liberation. Let's observe when these feelings arise inside us. What are they telling us? What aspect of ourselves or our lives are we comparing with others? When becoming aware of these patterns, we can begin to untangle them and free ourselves from their toxic influence.

Instead of competing with others, let's learn to compete with ourselves, creating challenges and goals to achieve. Practicing humility, we embrace our path without the need to compare ourselves with anyone else.

Envy, that dark shadow lurking in our soul's corner, is a powerful emotion that can undermine our happiness and inner peace. It arises when we compare our life with that of others and feel we are being left behind or lacking something they have.

But, like all emotions, envy can be a valuable sign.

When we feel envious, we are identifying a deep desire or longing. It shows us what we value and want in our lives. Instead of succumbing to envy, we can use it as an internal compass. Let's ask ourselves: What is this envy telling me? What can I do to get closer to what I crave instead of comparing myself to others?

By addressing envy this way, we turn a negative emotion into a tool for personal growth. We could learn to celebrate the successes of others and, at the same time, take measures to achieve our own goals. Envy reminds us that we are constantly evolving, capable of changing and growing. Let's take advantage of this lesson and transform envy into an engine of self-discovery and personal fulfillment.

Releasing Presumptiveness and Arrogance

Presumptuousness and arrogance construct walls around our ego, hindering humility. Identifying these traits requires courage and self-awareness. When we feel superior, we separate ourselves from shared humanity. Instead of rising above ourselves, let's practice empathy and understanding. True greatness lies in humility and the ability to learn from others, transcending status or position. By releasing presumptuousness and arrogance, we weave meaningful connections in our lives.

Impact on Mental Health

Arrogance, envy, and other destructive patterns burden our mental health, clouding our perception and distancing us from inner peace. Recognizing and addressing these emotions pave the way for robust mental health. *Cultivating humility, empathy, and understanding brings us closer to inner peace and strengthens relationships.*
Remember, you are not alone in this journey; we all face similar challenges. By releasing this burden, we open up space for healing and personal growth—creating a path to a healthier mind.

Humility is like the fertile soil that allows the most beautiful flowers to grow. To cultivate it, let's remember the metaphor of bamboo. As it grows, it bends its leaves to the ground in a gesture of humility. However, it continues to grow towards the sky. Likewise, by practicing humility, we incline our hearts towards humility, but we continue to grow in love, authenticity, and wisdom. Being authentic, noble, and generous, we nourish the roots of our souls and flourish as genuinely humble, unique, and unrepeatable beings.

Quantum Healing Practices: Transforming Your Well-Being

In this section, we immerse ourselves into the enchanting realm of quantum healing, where the mind and energy wield direct influence over health and well-being. These practices guide you on an odyssey toward physical, emotional, and spiritual healing.

Self-Healing: Captain of Your Destiny

Your journey to becoming the captain of your destiny unfolds through the mastery of self-healing. Within you lies the power to relieve pain, reduce stress, and manifest vitality. Like the regenerative salamander, you learn to rejuvenate and defy the constraints of time and aging. This intimate dance with your deepest being transforms you into the author of your own healing narrative.

My journey of self-healing is accompanied by miraculous transformations—testimonies of healing abound, defying medical and human understanding. Astonishing stories unfold from people that sought my help—revealing the inexplicable and the miraculous to the human understanding.

Visualization and Cellular Communication

Your body, a harmonious community of billions of cells, invites you to communicate through visualization and conscious intent. In this process, you embark on a ritual of communication with your cells, fostering optimal health and balance.

As part of this process, I will guide you through a simple ritual of self-communication with your cells; this conscious act will allow you to strengthen the connection between mind and body—promoting a flowing communication that will contribute to your well-being.

Preparation:
Find a quiet, distraction-free place to sit or lie down comfortably.

Deep Breathing:
Begin with deep breaths to induce relaxation. Close your eyes if desired, attune to the rhythm of your breathing.

Visualization:
Envision a warm, healing light radiating from your

heart, permeating your entire body. This light symbolizes your intent to heal and communicate with your cells.

Mental Contact:
Mentally reach out to your cells, establishing a connection. Say in your mind, "Every cell in my body, listen to me." Feel the connection with each cell.

Internal Dialogue:
Speak to your cells, expressing support and gratitude. "I'm here to care for and support you. Thank you for keeping me healthy. Together, we can achieve harmony and optimal health."

Creative Imagination:
Visualize your cells responding positively, working as a team to maintain balance and health in your body.

Gratitude:
Express gratitude to your cells for their continuous work. "Thank you, dear cells, for everything you do for me."

Completion:
Gradually return to awareness of your surroundings. Open your eyes if closed.

This journey into quantum healing practices empowers you to be the architect of your well-being. From self-healing miracles to cellular communication, these practices unveil the extraordinary potential within, guiding you toward physical, emotional, and spiritual harmony. As you continue this exploration, remember that your healing journey is a unique narrative, interwoven with the magic of quantum possibilities.

Quantum Healing at a Distance

Just as in our self-healing ritual through cellular communication, you can now become a channel of love and healing for those in need. Visualize the person, send positive thoughts, and healing energy with conscious intention. Love and intention transcend any distance, sparking profound healing processes. You now hold a potent tool to offer love and support to others, adapting the ritual to benefit and heal fellow beings. Trust in the power of your intention!

Healing Through Water

Delving deeper into quantum healing, we encounter an approach that has captivated global attention. Japanese scientist Masaru Emoto's groundbreaking work reveals the fascinating connection between water and healing. Emoto demonstrated how thoughts, emotions, and vibrations can influence water's structure.

This raises intriguing questions about how our intentions and emotions might positively impact our predominantly water-based bodies.

Quantum healing unfolds the deep connection between mind and matter, shedding light on holistic healing and our potential as conscious beings.

The Wonder of Water with Love

The remarkable power of water unveils a world of possibilities. Conscious use of this relationship with water becomes a tool for personal and collective benefit.
Infusing water with love and gratitude emerges as a simple yet potent healing practice. Imagine sipping water charged with the essence of positive intentions—an everyday act transformed into a powerful healing ritual.

Consider incorporating this practice into your daily life, blessing your water with love and positive energy, and sharing this blessed water to contribute to others' well-being.

Quantum healing teaches us that we transcend physical bodies, evolving as vibrant beings of energy and consciousness. As we deepen this understanding, our intentions and emotions emerge as potent influencers, even shaping the water we drink.

Art as a Healing Therapy: Artherapy

Art emerges as a formidable tool for healing the mind and body. Unleash your artistic and creative talents to find serenity and joy in daily life.

Discover Your Inner Artist
Dare to explore various artistic expressions—painting, drawing, writing, music, dance, cooking, or crafts. Art immerses you in the present, connecting you with your creative self.

The Power of Colors and Music
Colors and music possess the ability to influence emotions and moods. Learn to consciously use them to enhance emotional well-being and creativity.

My Personal Experience
As an artist, I've witnessed how art can heal and nourish the soul. The blank canvas transforms into an emotional refuge, infusing life, colors, and harmony into my existence. With a brushstroke, a dance, or a culinary creation, my world changes, and I renew myself inside and out.

Encouraging Your Artistic Vein

Here, I offer practices to inspire exploration of your artistic side. Whether drawing abstract lines, observing surroundings, waiting for serendipities, immersing in music, or cooking mindfully, these practices encourage the creative process.

The Magic of a Brush
Even without traditional artistic tools, creating art with simple materials can be an enriching ex-

perience. It's not about expertise but about enjoying the process. Discover the artist within and experience Artherapy, where colors, music, and creativity become tools for healing and happiness.

How to Encourage Your Artistic Vein
Your inner artist can flourish anywhere, anytime. Fan the flame of your creativity with these approaches:

> *Explore with Pencil and Paper:* Start with simple lines and strokes. Allow mistakes, and let intuition guide you.
>
> *Observe Your Surroundings:* Inspiration often lies in everyday life. Find beauty in colors, shapes, and textures around you.
>
> *Wait for Serendipities:* Creativity often arises unexpectedly. Stay alert for moments guiding your artistic journey.
>
> *The Magic of Music:* Let melodies inspire you. Sing or dance to unleash creativity.
>
> *Cooking with Awareness:* Cooking is an art form. Cook mindfully, savoring each ingredient, colors, and aromas for an enriching experience.

The Magic of a Brush: Creating Art by Yourself

You don't need to be a professional artist to create meaningful art. Begin your artistic journey with simple materials:

Gather Your Materials: Paper and colored pencils are enough to start. Choose colors that appeal to you. For more, learn to create paintings using simple spices from your kitchen.

Unleash Your Creativity: Find a quiet place, take a deep breath, and release tension.
Start drawing lines and shapes on the paper.
Don't worry about the final result; this is personal expression.

Be Observant: Observe the colors and how they mix on the paper. Explore and experiment.

Let Your Imagination Fly: Be carried away by your imagination. What emotions or thoughts arise during your creation?

Enjoy the Process: Beauty lies in the process as much as the result. Embrace your ability to create and relish every moment.

Your talent is waiting to be discovered on this planet surrounded by beauty. Colors, music, and creativity converge in this journey of self-discovery and healing. Discover how these exercises can enhance your life, providing a lasting sense of well-being.

38

The Butterfly Effect

Wings to Fly

"Patience is the companion of change, and every moment of waiting is an opportunity to grow"

The Butterfly Effect

The Butterfly Effect emerges in the depths of transformation, at the core of metamorphosis. It is a phenomenon that unfolds on the wings of consciousness and extends through each of us's inner universe.
What is the Butterfly Effect? It is the power of choice, the impulse of action, and the magnificence of manifestation. It is the belief in possibility, the certainty that every small choice, every seemingly insignificant act, can trigger a monumental change in our reality.

Precisely as a butterfly flapping her wings in a remote corner of the world can set off a chain of events that triggers a storm somewhere else, our daily choices and actions have an impact far beyond what we can imagine.

This chapter is a tribute to the Butterfly Effect that exists within you—It reminds you that every thought, emotion, and step you take creates an echo in the vast universe of your life. Every small choice is a seed that can grow into a tree of possibilities.
Today, I invite you to spread your wings and fly toward a future full of infinite possibilities. In this chapter, we will explore the art of conscious manifestation, the magic of co-creation, and the wisdom of patience. We will learn to trust the transformation process and embrace each stage of our journey. So, dear reader, prepare your wings and let yourself be carried by the wind of your dreams. Discover how every choice, no matter how small, can take us one step closer to the life we want. Today, I invite you to experience the Butterfly Effect in your own life.

The Wisdom of Patience

Patience is a great virtue that we often underestimate in our modern society. We live in a world of immediacy, where instant gratification has become the norm. However, in the journey of transformation and self-discovery, patience becomes a fundamental ally.

Imagine the caterpillar in its chrysalis, patiently waiting for its moment of transformation. Profound and surprising changes occur within you, but these processes take time.

The chrysalis does not open hastily; it waits until all the elements are in place and all the transformations have occurred before releasing the butterfly into the world.

Similarly, our lives are filled with chrysalis moments. They are moments in which we are in transition, in which we are changing, although we cannot always see it at that moment. In those moments, patience becomes our closest ally.

Patience does not mean immobility. It doesn't mean standing still and doing nothing. It means trusting life's process and innate wisdom to take us where we need to go. It means taking action, but it also means understanding that some things take time to develop fully.

On this page, we are looking at the importance of patience in our transformation journey. We will learn to trust the rhythm of life and allow ourselves to be, even when we do not see immediate results. We will discover how patience can be the key to unlocking doors we never imagined. The wisdom of patience is the guide that takes us through the stages of our transformation process.

So, as you embark on this journey, remember the lesson of the caterpillar in its chrysalis: — "Patience is the companion of change, and every moment of waiting is an opportunity to grow."

The freedom of transformation

As we move forward on our transformation journey, we realize that transformation is ultimately liberation. It is the freedom to be who we really are and to let go of the limitations that we impose on ourselves or that society has imposed on us.

Imagine the butterfly just emerging from its chrysalis. Her wings spread, vibrant and beautiful. Finally, she is free to explore the vast world around her. In its previous form as a caterpillar, its movements were limited. But now, like a butterfly, you have the freedom to fly and go wherever you want.

Likewise, when we embrace transformation in our lives, we free ourselves from self-imposed limitations. We certainly realize that we have been living in an invisible chrysalis of fears, limiting beliefs, and doubts. We become the butterfly we have always been inside by freeing ourselves from these mental and emotional ties.

The freedom of transformation invites us to be authentic, to live courageously, and to explore our passions and purposes with joy. It encourages us to fly towards new horizons, face challenges confidently, and embrace each day as an opportunity to grow and expand.

In this final chapter of our journey, we will celebrate the freedom that transformation offers us. We will discover how to release our inner wings and embrace life with a renewed sense of wonder and gratitude. Like the butterfly that soars in the sky, we, too, are capable of rising to new heights on our path of transformation.

So, dear reader, prepare to fly, embrace the freedom of transformation, and live life in all its splendor. The journey continues, and each day is an opportunity to discover your potential and live a life that fills you with joy and meaning.

To conclude this chapter, I want to remind you of a fundamental idea: transformation is a continuous process. No matter what stage of your life you are in, you always have the power to transform and grow.

The butterfly does not stop flying once it leaves its chrysalis; it continues to explore the world and adapt to new challenges.

So, as you embark on your very own metamorphosis journey, remember to be kind to yourself. Patience, acceptance, and self-love are powerful allies on this path. No matter how many obstacles you encounter, you have the inner strength to overcome them and continue evolving.

39

The New You

The Metamorphosis

"Life brims with endless possibilities, and you are the sorcerer of your destiny"

As you delve into the practices and wisdom within this book, you're embarking on a profound journey of transformation—your evolution. Unveiling the mysteries of the mind and heart, exploring Quantum Psychology's power, and mastering the art of healing emotions, you've gained a deeper understanding of yourself and the universe.

This book isn't the conclusion of your journey; it's a commencement. Armed with tools and insights, your ability to apply these teachings in your daily life is the true key. Always remember, you're the architect of your reality. Exploring the quantum facets of your being, you'll discover the power to reshape your life in unimaginable ways.

Life brims with endless possibilities, and you are the sorcerer of your destiny.

I urge you to persist in your exploration, never ceasing to learn and grow. Keep the flame of curiosity alive, ceaselessly unraveling the wonders of your mind and heart. Life unfolds as a continuous odyssey of self-discovery, and I'm thrilled you've chosen to partake in it.

In moments of uncertainty or adversity, let the words of this book echo within you, a reminder of the potent force dwelling within. You possess the capability to lead an extraordinary life filled with joy, purpose, and authenticity. Seize the opportunity to craft the life you rightfully deserve.

We are Stardust
Live out the magic to its fullest, wield your enchanting wand

Epilogue

Every word etched on these pages is a stroke on the canvas of your soul, a note in the symphony of your life, a mark on the road to transformation. From the depths of quantum reality to the pinnacles of consciousness, you've navigated the mysteries of the universe and the marvels of your existence.

This book has been a voyage of revelation, a gentle nudge that you are the co-author of your reality—a vastly powerful being capable of manifesting your deepest aspirations. Patience has been your guiding light, challenges regarded as stepping stones, and transformation recognized as a beautiful process necessitating time and care.

As you close these pages, carry the lessons of this journey with you. Embrace the wisdom of patience, trust the process of transformation, and always remember that you possess the wings to soar toward your dreams. This book is merely the inception. Your narrative, your expedition, and your transformation continue. And as you bid farewell to these words, acknowledge that you're ushering in a new chapter, one teeming with boundless possibilities.

Thank you for sharing this odyssey with me until our next rendezvous—where we'll persist in unraveling the universe's mysteries and exploring the enchantment of your being.

With wings unfurled,

Miliza De Soto

Feel free to reach out with any queries or reflections or drop a comment.

miliza@milizadesoto.com
eureka@milizadesoto.com

In Honor of Those Who Illuminated My Path

I've reached the end of this journey, where I've been able to materialize a dream—something I didn't plan this way but already existed in my own handwriting. I give thanks to all those who made it possible, who have been instruments to play this melody full of magic. Each one has played a note of this score—now I have my complete symphony.

This is my profound gratitude to each one who reminded me that I had to share my humble words and help through my literary voice—reaching many hearts. Here I am today, brimming with emotions, to say that I saw all the signs—a grand serendipity shook my being, and with a shower of magical epiphanies, I understood what I had to do. My unforgettable 'Eureka' moments.

My father, my eternal inspiration, who has witnessed my growth since I was a child and encouraged me to share with my written voice. Always proud of me, I give you what you've asked for so long. Grazie mille, tua piccolina.

Alejandro, thank you for inspiring me and for all your support in this wonderful journey.

Laura, your help in transcribing my notes marked the beginning of all this. Thanks for your trust, motivation, and presence. We are cosmic sisters, stardust.

Johanna, who has always believed in me, listens to and laughs at so much profound information—no one like you to listen to me. Undoubtedly, this book is as much yours as mine. Thank you for believing in me, for waiting for it, and for supporting me—our connection with the cosmos is magical and eternal.

AJ, our deep conversations and sharing my writings were always very special. You have been my motivation and pride—and always will be 444. Thanks for your support and inspiration.

Clemen, your words always resonated with me—it was my cornerstone. Infinite thanks, and I also want to recognize your dad, Dr. Vallès, my dear teacher and my other father, whose teachings in medicine left a deep impression on me. I'm sure he's proud wherever he is.

Jose Antonio, my favorite guinea pig, who always supports me in my adventures and experiments, who believes in me and never doubts. Thanks for helping me so much and for all your medical knowledge—you're the best radiologist.

Paul, my cosmic twin, thank you for always being there, for supporting me in all my ideas and creations, for believing in me, and giving me more inspiration. Let's continue with those magical fingers.

Chris, thank you so much for all your help, support, feedback, and brilliant ideas—it is always above and beyond. I can't thank you enough.

Ciara, my colleague and former partner, you trusted me without hesitation and managed to see my purpose—this compendium is one more result—always grateful. Molt bé papallona.

Nelson, infinite thanks for sharing your experiences as an author, for the support, and for those tips that I've valued and followed.

Cesar, my gratitude is infinite for your dedication and unconditional help; your great talent I see in each of my creations. Your patience and creativity are a gift to me—you're a magnificent designer and a great human being—thanks for your presence and for your help in creating this book and the beautiful website.

Alberto, thank you very much for your help, for your talent and experience that is reflected in each page of this manuscript. You are part of the team and the magic.

Carol, thank you for your dedicated work, for editing so wonderfully, and for becoming part of my magical journey.

Greys, my gratitude is so immense for all your support, believing in me, and always saying something so beautiful. It is an honor to be your inspiration and pride.

Beatriz, thank you for each and every word of wisdom; they were the magical touch.

Jeannine, thanks to infinity, you're my other cornerstone and who listens to me and always trusts me for valuing and inspiring me at every step of my journey.

Julia, thank you for all your support and help and for being so proud of me. My love and gratitude are "to infinity and beyond."

My dear family, to my mother and my siblings, thanks for the unconditional love and support.

Lola, thanks for so many deep conversations, our eternal and wise discussions, you're my light, Mom's pride, and my inspiration.

And to my Nicky, happy and proud of his mom, thanks for your support, for inspiring me, for your love and wisdom. This book is yours too.

My gratitude is eternal, full of love and deep respect,

Miliza

"In every word of gratitude, in every dedicated memory, the eternal glow of the souls who have woven the tapestry of my existence is revealed. In their light, I find the reflection of my own being. In their love, I discover the strength to move forward.
With every brushstroke of gratitude, I write a poem of entwined souls, a tribute to the symphony of life."

—Miliza De Soto"

The Author

The Visionary Explorer of the Mind and Energy

From her early days, Miliza showed an innate love for understanding how the world around her works. With an inquisitive mind, he began his search for answers to fundamental questions about life, consciousness and reality.

Her journey of exploration commenced in her youth and meandered through diverse realms of academic and self-directed studies. From delving into the sciences and philosophy to expressing herself through art, dance, and writing, Miliza's quest for knowledge has been multifaceted.

Armed with extensive experience and years of dedicated study in mind and energy sciences, Miliza De Soto has emerged as a passionate explorer of the mysteries of the mind. Her unique narrative weaves together insights from various disciplines, reflecting her creative and holistic approach to life.

Beyond her intellectual pursuits, Miliza thrives as a businesswoman in the world of olive oil and Mediterranean products. Her creative focus permeates every aspect of her life, integrating her diverse interests into a harmonious whole.

Miliza's love for the arts, coupled with her commitment to self-discovery and quantum healing, has enabled her to positively impact the lives of many. Her activities and explorations mirror a continuous quest for personal and collective growth.

This book stands as a testament to Miliza's dedication, offering a gift to those seeking a deeper understanding of the power of the mind and energy. Her biography is a celebration of the human spirit's innate capacity for achieving the seemingly unattainable—a story of discovery and a tribute to the limitless potential within each of us.

"In every quest for the truth, we find a glimpse of our most authentic being."
—Miliza

Contributions and Influences

Masters and Inspirations

Paracelsus, Hermes Trismegistus, Nikola Tesla, David Bohm, Max Planck, Leonardo da Vinci, Neville Goddard, Stephen Hawking, Carl Jung, Fibonacci, William Walker Atkinson, William James, Ernest Holmes, Niels Bohr, Roger Penrose, Nicolas Flamel, Isaac Newton, Frank Herbert, among others, have left indelible marks on my quest for knowledge and creation.

These great masters have been my source of inspiration and illuminated the path of my scientific and spiritual exploration. Through their teachings, they have led me to discover the great secrets of the mind and the universe in ways I could never have imagined.

Every page of their works has brought me closer to my true passion: the exploration of the mind and energy. Each word they have written, each idea they have shared, has been like a key that opened the doors to understanding and co-creation in my life.

The 'Eureka' moments I experienced whilst reading their works have become cornerstones in my journey.

Every revelation I found in their writings propelled me beyond the limits of my knowledge and inspired me to apply their teachings in my daily life.
This tribute is my humble way of expressing deep gratitude to these masters. Through their words and wisdom, I have found my voice as a scientist, exploring the mind and energy. I pay homage to them for guiding and teaching me to consciously and lovingly co-create my reality.

The rebellious and visionary alchemist Paracelsus showed me the path to internal transmutation. Through his writings, I discovered the power of transformation and renewal, remembering that true magic lies in the art of turning lead into gold, both in the body and the spirit. His teachings have left an indelible mark on my journey, reminding me that the alchemy of life lies in the constant process of turning adversity into growth and darkness into light.

With his timeless wisdom, Hermes Trismegistus whispered to me the magic of correspondence, reminding me that each experience reflects an echo in the universe. Through his teachings, I embraced the connection between the earthly and the divine, finding the resonance of the infinite in every moment.

With his holistic approach, David Bohm led me hand in hand toward understanding the cosmic dance that governs our existence. His words showed me the beauty of totality, the subtle choreography weaving our lives into a tapestry of infinite interconnections.

I conclude with the perspective of the great Nikola Tesla on energy and the secret of the universe; with his avant-garde vision—he illuminated me with the revelation of the omnipresent energy that surrounds us. Following in his footsteps, I learned to listen to the whispers of the universe in the electric current of life, recognizing the divine spark that unites all creation and understanding energy from a quantum and holistic perspective—his ideas encouraged me to consider energy not only as a physical force but as a more subtle expression of universal consciousness.

Each of these masters became a beacon on my journey, guiding me through the darkness of knowledge and exploration. Their lessons transcended the boundaries of the physical and intellectual, weaving in me a deeper understanding and an eternal connection with the vastness of the cosmos.

With eternal gratitude, I share these moments of inspiration with my readers, hoping that they, too, find the path to a more conscious and fulfilling life in these teachings.

References and Consultations:
Real Academia de la Lengua Española Dictionary
Cambridge Dictionary

Contents

Prologue 5
Dedication 9
Introduction 11
Fundamentals of Quantum Alchemy 13

1. The Power of Consciousness 17
2. A Coherent Signal 19
3. Inner Illumination 21
4. Life by Design 23
5. Learning to Let Go 27
6. Physics of Consciousness 29
7. The Key to Conscious Creation 33
8. The Magic of Anticipation 35
9. The Quantum Dance 37
10. The Power of Cognition and Imagination ... 41
11. The Power of Focus and Belief 45
12. The Power of Expectation and the New Reality 49
13. Quantum Surprises 53
14. The Energy of Atoms 55
15. The Symphony of Being 59
16. The Physics of Consciousness 63
17. The Science of Consciousness 67
18. Quantum Law 69
19. The Law of Thought Vibration 73
20. The Magic of Gratitude and Reception 77
21. The Science of Consciousness and Quantum Physics ... 81

22. The Journey to Self-Realization 85
23. The Path of Self-Transcendence 87
24. The Dance of Co-Creation 89
25. The Creation of a New Reality 91
26. Embracing Inner Power 95
27. The Path to Mastery 99
28. Living in Harmony 101
29. Quantum Law 103
30. The Exploration of Self 107
31. Unity in Diversity 111
32. Free Will and Destiny 115
33. Serendipities and Epiphanies 121
34. The Superpower of the Subconscious Mind 133
35. Beyond Reality 163
36. Quantum Psychology 173
37. Quantum Healing and Energy Psychology 181
38. The Butterfly Effect 211
39. The New You 217

Epilogue 219

www.ingramcontent.com/pod-product-compliance
Lightning Source LLC
Chambersburg PA
CBHW060507090426
42735CB00011B/2140